GLASS

Philosophy and Method

JOHN BURTON

Hand-Blown

Sculptured

Colored

BONANZA BOOKS · NEW YORK

To Elsie, my wife, who shares
all my adventures in glass

Copyright © MCMLXVII by John Burton
Library Of Congress Catalog Card Number: 67-28894
All rights reserved.
This edition is published by Bonanza Books
a division of Crown Publishers, Inc.
by arrangement with the author
a   b   c   d   e   f   g   h
Manufactured in the United States Of America

Foreword

It is always a great event, and a somewhat rare one, when an artist-craftsman of distinguished achievement sets out to share his unique creative techniques with the rest of us, who may have applauded his work for years while wondering just how his seemingly impossible effects were produced.

With simple clarity of word, line drawing, and superb photography, my friend John Burton has done just that in this book. He has made possible for others a new and fascinating creative adventure with glass—in the classroom of any school or university, and, perhaps most importantly, in the home, by anyone who is drawn to fill a part of his increasing leisure time exploring a new field that offers limitless possibilities for achievement.

But this is much more than a book of technical instruction—it is the warm, imaginative, human document of a world traveler in search of the best that others have achieved in his own chosen medium, glass, through the three-and-a-half millennia since the Egyptians first formed the glass treasures that now adorn our museums.

Though the long romantic history of glass—"the supreme chalice for light and color," as John Burton calls it—cannot be told in a single book, here he tells enough to whet the appetite for more. He tells it as a lover of art embarked on a voyage of discovery. His simple words paint unforgettable images in the mind and heart, as beautiful as his own three-dimensional glass creations, when he speaks of the deep meaning of individual creativity linked eternally to the ever-changing masterpiece that surrounds man in his nature cradle.

Perhaps the building of new worlds must always begin with the pioneer who accepts the challenge to clothe his creative vision in new forms, be they large or small. "He and his creation are one," Burton tells us. "This is himself at full stretch, in full action. This is his to do, his unique private enterprise, a giving of his best to the man-made world. His total being is alive, and knows the joy of active engagement in the fulfillment of his singleness of purpose. This is his spontaneous way of life, for which there is no substitute."

I am delighted and honored to express my hearty appreciation of this important work. I wish it, and its author, Godspeed.

AILEEN O. WEBB
Chairman of the Board,
The American Craftsmen's Council

President,
The World Crafts Council

Author's Note

This is a book about people and glass—in that order. More particularly, about you or me and glass. Glass objects cannot read books—we can. This means that we are the masters, and glass is our servant. We can mold it to our purposes.

Writing in 1751 in his famous magazine, *The Rambler*, Samuel Johnson paid this striking tribute to glass:

Who, when he first saw the sand and ashes by casual intenseness of heat melted into a metalline form, rugged with excrescenses and clouded with impurities, would have imagined that in this shapeless lump lay concealed so many conveniences of life as would in time constitute a great part of the happiness of the world? Yet by some such fortuitous liquefaction was mankind taught to procure a body at once in a high degree solid and transparent, which might admit the light of the sun and exclude the violence of the wind, which might extend the sight of the philosopher to new ranges of existence, and charm him at one time with the unbounded extent of the material creation, and at another with the endless subordination of animal life and, what is yet of more importance, might supply the decay of nature and succor old age with subsidiary sight. Thus was

the first artificer of glass employed though without his own knowl-
edge or expectation. He was facilitating and prolonging the enjoy-
ments of light, enlarging the avenues of science, and conferring the
highest and most lasting pleasures; he was enabling the student to
contemplate nature, and the beauty to behold herself.

Samuel Johnson was a man of great vision. We are living now in
what I call the Age of Glass. What follows in this book is intended
as an invitation to you to come to know glass by taking it into your
hands in your own home, school, university, or recreation club, and
learning to manipulate it according to your own creative imagination into new forms that do honor to its native beauty as the supreme
transmitter of light and color.

When the artist-craftsman dreams of a thing of beauty, and then
proceeds with his own skillful hands so to manipulate his medium
that the dream, more or less successfully, becomes clothed with
objective reality, love of his work is the mainspring that motivates
and guides him through the self-discipline that all creative effort
demands.

He and his creation are one. This is himself at full stretch, in full
action. This is his to do, his unique private enterprise, a giving of
his best to the man-made world. His total being is alive, and knows
the joy of active engagement in the fulfillment of his singleness of
purpose. This is his spontaneous way of life, for which there is no
substitute.

Nor does this creative mood desert him when he leaves his workshop. It comes to dominate his waking hours. Everywhere he is a
man dignified by the fulfillment of his inner calling, a man whose
vision and work align him with the striving of all men of goodwill
for individual freedom and obedience to just laws. His work is also
his greatest pleasure, and through it he re-creates himself perpetu-
ally, blessed with the peace of mind that rewards the creator. With
his work he delights himself and his friends, and may come to
delight a small or wide unknown group of his fellows in his state
or nation.

Author's Note

Implicit in a society built on the worth of the individual, on law and justice, is this freedom of every man to live and work at his unique creative best. Men are not alike, nor is there equal vigor and talent in them. Freedom to function, each in his own way, within the laws that make for harmony in human society leads to what John Ruskin called "the harmonious inequality of concurrent power." I know of no six words that better describe the relatedness of men who would keep their individual and national orbits clear of chaos.

Acknowledgments

I want to express my gratitude to the many close friends who have helped and encouraged me during the lengthy preparation of this book. My special thanks go to our great friend Rein Bredius for the long hours of patient skillful work she has devoted to making the diagrams and line sketches of my models; also, to my photographer friends John Weir, Jerry Predika, Guy Raymond Coté, Thomas Schwab, and Nora Klinjan who so ably prepared many of the black and white pictures and color plates.

I am deeply grateful to Mrs. Aileen O. Webb, Chairman of the Board of the American Craftsmen's Council and President of the World Crafts Council, for her great understanding and help through many years of friendship; to Dr. Henry Allen Moe, former President of the Guggenheim Foundation, for his friendship and inspired encouragement at all times; to Mr. Paul N. Perrot, Director of the Corning Museum of Glass, Corning, N.Y., for his invaluable suggestions as connoisseur and historian of glass; to Mr. Hugh Wakefield, Keeper of Circulation at the Victoria and Albert Museum in London, who has cheered us on during our research travels in Europe.

Introduction

A deep awareness of one of society's growing problems—unexploited leisure time—and a profound understanding of man's instinctive desire to make things which he can truly call his own, have led John Burton into a most individual exploration of glass as a medium of creative expression. This volume is not a treatise expounding methodology for its own sake, rather is it the presentation of a philosophy toward work and life, which, in his case, has taken tangible form in his passion for glass.

In exploring this brilliant and paradoxical substance which can be at will massive or eggshell thin, soft or sharp, infinitely colored or air clear, he has found solace and personal fulfillment. He has discovered and come to terms with its rules and limitations, and adapted them so that they are now the gentle vehicle for his fancy and delight.

In this book he attempts to impart for the first time, to a nonspecialized audience, the principles of an age-old technique. He shows how it can be developed within the privacy of one's home at little cost, and that with imagination, patience, and even a modicum of talent a host of useful and evocative forms can be produced. John

Burton does not address himself to the technologist, who deals with the raw ingredients of glass and its innumerable scientific properties and uses, nor to the glass historian, whose main interest must always lie in the past. Rather, he aims at either those who, fascinated by the beauty and unique properties of glass, are waiting only for practical guidance to begin a creative adventure of their own, or those for whom the daily rush of living culminates in the contemplation of those fearful days of retirement, and to whom he offers a new method of rewarding self-expression.

Lampworking is only one of the varied aspects of glassmaking which the individual craftsman can exploit. It is, however, particularly suited to the needs of those who wish to explore this magical metal, and find, in their own idiom, expression for their fancy. Let us hope that other guides will follow from the hand of those increasingly numerous artist-craftsmen for whom the mystery of glass lies in the pot rather than in the torch. In time, no doubt, they will make their contribution to the art of glassmaking. But their guides will not take the place of, or even compete with, the direction suggested by John Burton, for, according to his philosophy, the search is more important than the result, and the permanent contribution is to be found not so much in the object made as in what making the object has meant to its creator.

PAUL N. PERROT
Director, The Corning Museum of Glass
Corning Glass Center
Corning, New York

Contents

"When men are rightly occupied, their amusement grows out of their work, as the colour-petals out of a fruitful flower."—JOHN RUSKIN

PART I

A BEGINNING

Ancient peoples have written some of their most revealing history in glass; today, modern people are doing the same thing in ever greater measure. If some cataclysm should engulf our cities, future archaeologists would find everything from beer bottles to skyscrapers made of glass. They would find telescopes and microscopes and shattered glass laboratory equipment—the very instruments and implements that made twentieth-century science possible and gave us our fantastic technological world.

Glass, with its incredibly versatile properties, has invaded every area of scientific research and conquest, and has become so much a part of our every-day home life that it almost seems to belong to the natural world, like the lumber in our houses. But glass is not a part of the natural world. It was first made by man from common ingredients that lie all about us in nature, but that was so long ago that neither the time nor the place is known. Historians and archaeologists are generally agreed that the first sure evidence of continuous glassmaking dates from about thirty-five hundred years ago in Egypt. Those were humble beginnings. The blowpipe was not invented until fifteen hundred years later. Yet the Egyptians of the New Kingdom devised ingenious ways of forming hollow glass around a sand core attached to the end of a metal or wooden rod. Of course, the sand had to be removed later—no easy task! But with such primitive methods they created pieces that rank high among the world's art treasures.

Today, the word "glass" is no more than a generic term, covering the thousands of different glasses now being manufactured for scientific and industrial uses. It is, perhaps, not too much to say that without this miracle-making substance we should still be back in the Dark Ages struggling to attain the light. Imagine, if you can, a world with no glass windows, no electric light, no radio or television, no spectacles, no motor cars or airplanes, no motion pictures! The list is long.

We have had our Stone, Bronze, and Iron Ages; now we have what might be called the Glass Age in which are foreshadowed huge buildings, perhaps whole cities, fabricated with structural glass, which is noncorrosive and stronger, lighter, and far less costly than steel. A visit to the Corning Glass Center at Corning, New York, provides a hint of what is possible. There you will see one of the twenty-ton discs of Pyrex glass cast for the mirror of the 200-inch telescope at Mount Palomar in California—the largest single glass item ever made. You will see an array of huge glass pipes, with twists and turns, couplings and valves—an almost endless variety of glass equipment for performing the modern miracles of chemistry. On film you can see molten glass pour in a thin ribbon from an automatically fed furnace at twenty-five miles an hour, or more, and be formed into perfect glass tubing, and can watch the

20

automatic machinery that fashions the TV picture tubes we gaze at in our homes.

But such giant achievements we must rightly leave to industrial engineers. Our interest, in the chapters that lie ahead, will center on glass as a medium for the artist-craftsman. Here you will find a carefully detailed and illustrated guide which will enable you to master the unique methods I have evolved and practiced in my own home for more than twenty years, even though you have had no previous experience, and I shall hope that blowing, sculpting, and forming glass may come to be for you what it is for me—the most exciting and rewarding creative work with the hands that I know.

JOHN BURTON
Santa Barbara, California

CHAPTER 1

Initiation into the World of Glass

My earliest memory of the magic ritual of blowing and manipulating red-hot glass takes me back to Holland. Still in my early twenties, I was a guest one summer in the charming home of my friend, Mynheer Marijn Cochius, who presided over the world-famous Glasfabriek at Leerdam, near Utrecht.

The day after my arrival we walked together through brilliant sunshine from his old-world house to the nearby factory, passing through a small side door into what seemed to be a stone cave. I stood rooted to the spot. Was this a dream, or was it real?

A lurid orange light spread from three stationary circles in a blackened wall. Three dancing balls of fire floated through the air, taking circular paths and then suddenly disappearing into the ground. As my eyes grew accustomed to the weird light, I saw that the fireballs were attached to the ends of long iron rods manipulated by three powerful men. The stationary circles were the mouths of furnaces. Each man was swinging his fireball over his head and down into a pit, making a complete circle, like a dancer of consummate skill performing some *cancan d'enfer* in a ritual of the Black Arts. Small wonder that, in the superstitious Middle Ages, when glassmakers were widely accorded great respect (and even envy), they sometimes were believed by the ignorant to be engaged in traffic with the Devil—perhaps putting their souls in pawn for Satanic guidance at the mouths of the fires of Hell.

My friend broke in on my reverie. "That takes skill!" he observed. I agreed.

The accompanying illustration, which I was fortunate enough to find in an antique shop in London, dates from 1850, and depicts an almost identical scene. Imagine, if you can, the degree of confidence each of the three men in the picture must have had in the other two! The slightest slip or miscalculation of a swing would have brought down many pounds of red-hot metal onto the next operator, with lethal results. I watched this same "dance" at Leerdam hour after hour, and never noticed the slightest hesitation in the performance, or any sign of apprehension on the part of the performers. Occasionally a little water, or saliva, was allowed to trickle through the blowpipe. The resulting steam made the huge

FIGURE 1. Manufacture of glass for "The Crystal Palace" at Messrs. Chance's Works, Spon-Lane, near Birmingham, England (1850).

THE

GUIDE TO KNOWLEDGE.

EDITED BY MR. W. PINNOCK,

AUTHOR OF "PINNOCK'S CATECHISMS," "GRAMMAR OF GEOGRAPHY AND HISTORY," ETC. ETC.

No. V.]   SUPPLEMENT, JULY 31, 1832.   ONE PENNY.

MANUFACTURE OF GLASS.

In the whole circle of our manufactures there is not any thing more curious than the one that is depicted in the above engraving. Materials which appear of themselves but little fitted for any useful purpose, are blended together so as to form compounds of a new and entirely distinct character. Indeed, an uninitiated person looking at the sand, lead, and pearl ashes, as they are prepared for the glass-house, would consider that nothing less than the wand of the enchanter could accomplish their change into a hard and crystalline body.

Our metropolis possesses but two large *Glass-houses*, as they are called, and they are both of them open to any person who requires any peculiarly formed vessel which is not commonly kept in their respective warehouses. One of them is in Water-lane, and the other at the south-side of Blackfriar's bridge. Now, we purpose in the first instance, to explain to our readers the general process of manufacturing glass, and then point out how, by a small and simple apparatus, any person may perform all the most important manipulations in this beautiful art.

The ingredients usually employed in the manufacture of glass, with their relative proportions, may be thus briefly described :

VOL. I.

120 parts of well-washed white sand		
40	„	purified pearl ashes
35	„	litharge
13	„	nitre
1	„	black oxide of manganese.

When these materials are collected and properly proportioned, they receive a certain amount of calcination prior to their being placed in the melting-pot. This operation is called *fritting*, and is performed either in small furnaces adjoining to the proper glass furnace, and heated by the same fuel, after its principal force has been expended on the glass-pots, or else in ovens constructed for the purpose. The use of this preparatory process is to discharge all moisture from the ingredients, and to drive off the carbonic gas. This operation is performed gradually, and carried to the point of semi-vitrification. When the materials are sufficiently "fritted," they are thrown with clean iron shovels, through the side opening of the furnace, into the glass-pots, the fire having been previously raised to its greatest intensity. When filled, the opening is closed with wet clay, excepting a small hole for examining the interior of the furnace. The mass soon begins to heave, and exhibit a mass

1

FIGURE 2. THE GUIDE TO KNOWLEDGE, 1932.

bubble expand as no pair of human lungs could have done. Large round bubbles made in this manner were later trepanned (cut out) to make "blanks" to be ground into spectacle lenses. Of course modern techniques have long since outmoded such old-world practices.

Since that dramatic introduction to a glass factory, I have watched the astonishing skills of glassworkers all over the world. Little has changed in the process of what is termed "offhand glassblowing," simply because no better methods have been found for producing the wide range of glass articles for the domestic market. In every country the process is still substantially the same, though what is produced is by no means of equal merit.

One hundred and thirty-five years ago, in London's famous *Guide to Knowledge*—price: one penny—appeared the brief description of glassmaking reproduced here in part. (See Fig. 2.) In broad outline the same process is in universal operation today.

FIGURE 3.

At the close of this article, reference is made to a Professor Partington and the simple heating device (see Fig. 3) he used in public lectures to show how glass can be blown or molded on a small scale. It is an ingenious device, and the professor undoubtedly made some successful demonstrations with it. For us it only serves to show the enormous changes that have taken place in laboratory equipment since the *Guide to Knowledge* appeared.

But even in 1832 such a device was not new. In 1612, Antonio Neri, an Italian priest, published his famous book, *Arte Vitraria*. Until that time, the theories and techniques of the glass art had re-

26

FIGURE 4. Reproduced from an illustration in a French translation
and adaptation of *Arte Vitraria*, by Antonio Neri, published by
Baron d'Holbach in 1752. *Courtesy, the Koninklijke Bibliotheek,
'S Gravenhage, Holland.*

FIGURE 5. Greek lamps.

mained cloaked in secrecy. Neri now brought the whole subject out into the open. Figure 4 is reproduced from an illustration in a French translation and adaptation of this rare work published by Baron d'Holbach in 1752. It shows three young women engaged in making glass beads. Forced air, provided by the foot bellows under the bench, is being directed through the small flame of an oil-burning lamp to soften a quantity of glass large enough to make a bead. But such a lamp was still a very late-comer in the long line of primitive oil-burning devices that date back to prehistoric times.

The oldest lamps were probably animal skulls filled with fats that burned through some kind of fiber wick. These, of course, were possible only after primitive man had learned to make fire by friction. Seashells were also used as fat or oil containers for lamps. Still later, stone and clay lamps began to appear, fashioned by human hands. My own small collection of clay lamps from Greece and Rome varies in age from about the fourth century B.C. to the second century A.D.

Next came metal lamps in enormous variety of size and design; a long succession of more efficient light producers, with better and

28

FIGURE 6. Roman cinerary urn and cover (late 1st century A.D.). *Courtesy, Victoria & Albert Museum, London, Crown Copyright.*

29

bigger wicks; graceful temple lamps, chased and enameled, or severe and plain; lamps for houses, lamps for indoor and outdoor workers. All had their hour and played their part as relatives on the family Lamp Tree. Examples of almost every kind ever made are still in use somewhere in the world.

But gas lamps were waiting around a few corners. Toward the middle of the nineteenth century Robert W. Bunsen came along with his first "Bunsen burner," and the "batswing" gas flame became the chief source of light in many homes in civilized Europe. Then came the incandescent mantle, relegating the "batswing burner" to the attic.

The Bunsen burner became the patriarch of a line that led to the development of the great range of torches in use today. First, jets of air were blown through the Bunsen flame to produce great heat in a small area, just as smaller jets of air were once blown through the tiny flame burning on the wick of the primitive oil lamp. This led to a single instrument that delivered both flammable gas and air under pressure to a mixing nozzle on the end of a metal tube, where ignition took place. Since that step was taken, improvement in design and efficiency has resulted in the many forms of versatile modern torches. I always find it amusing to hear people talk of work with the gas-oxygen torch as "lamp work." But that is still the accepted name for it, and it has come down from the supreme great-grandfather of all the devices that men have used through several millennia.

CHAPTER 2

Properties of Glass, Some Early History, and My Search for New Methods

Now that we have seen the dramatic manner in which glass was manipulated, and have recognized that it has unique plastic qualities, we are naturally curious to know what it is made of, who invented it, and where and when.

Today, the word "glass" covers thousands of widely differing substances, each having built-in properties for special kinds of services. All these substances, however, have characteristics in common, which mark them as glass regardless of their chemical composition.

The major ingredient of glass is silicon oxide (silica—SiO_2), with lesser amounts of lead, potassium, sodium, calcium, aluminum, and iron oxides. Not all of these oxides are necessarily found in any one glass. The chemistry of glass is a highly complicated scientific study, and the practical details of glass manufacture from a wide range of common elements lie outside our scope. Innumerable books on these subjects are available.

Perhaps the definition of G. W. Morey, the world-famous chemist, speaks most clearly of the unique behavior of this fascinating substance: "A glass is an inorganic substance in a condition which

Figure 7. Covered beaker attributed to Gottfried Spiller, Potsdam, Germany (c. 1700–1710). *Courtesy, The Corning Museum of Glass, Corning, N. Y.*

FIGURE 8. Covered sugar bowl of transparent pale bluish aqua-
marine glass. Redford or Redwood Glass Works, New York (c.
1835–1850). *Courtesy, The Corning Museum of Glass, Corning,
N. Y.*

FIGURE 9. Double-walled beaker with elaborate paper and straw scene representing the balloon ascent of V. Lunardi in Naples. Bachmetev Glasshouse, Russia (early 19th century). *Courtesy, The Corning Museum of Glass, Corning, N. Y.*

FIGURE 10. English wine glass (1581). *Courtesy, Victoria & Albert Museum, London, Crown Copyright.*

is continuous with, and analogous to, the liquid state of that substance, but which, as the result of having been cooled from a fused condition, has attained so high a degree of viscosity as to be for all practical purposes rigid."

Our senses tell us that the glass we hold in our hand is hard and solid. The glass we dropped on the stone floor tells us that it is also brittle. The chemist tells us that, despite these obvious facts, the glass from which you drink water is itself a liquid. These are some of the properties of cold glass.

FIGURE 11. English jug (c. 1675).
Courtesy, Victoria & Albert Museum, London, Crown Copyright.

When glass is heated to a high temperature, it gradually loses these properties. First it softens and becomes viscous, and, when the temperature is increased, it finally flows like water. We refer to glass as a metal, yet, unlike other metals, it has no definite melting point—only a softening point. Thereafter, as the heat is increased, it becomes less and less viscous and more and more fluid. It is while in the intermediate state of high viscosity that it can be blown and shaped in innumerable ways.

For our technical purposes, we shall be concerned with just one kind of glass, suited to the kind of creative work we have in mind. This is a borosilicate, known by the trade name "Pyrex." It is manufactured by the Corning Glass Company. Pyrex glass softens at about 850 degrees Centigrade, which is higher than the point at which the more common soda glass softens. It also has a low coefficient of expansion, which is to say that it expands relatively little when heated, and, conversely, contracts very little when cooled. These properties make it ideal for our work.

Who first created this strange substance called glass? No one has ever been able to answer that question with any certainty. Archaeologists, historians, and scientists have been able to do no more than pool and try to interpret their findings to supply us with educated guesses. Pliny, the Roman historian, writing at the beginning of the Christian era, relates that a company of merchants sailing their ship along the coast of Phoenicia dropped anchor and went ashore to cook their evening meal. Finding no stones on the beach, they brought blocks of natron (soda) from their cargo to support the cauldron over the fire. When the fire was at its hottest, the natron melted and combined with the sand, to produce the first man-made glass. True or not, the story is a good one, and such a fusion could have occurred. Actually, we are all more interested in plausible, colorful stories of the long ago than in so-called facts of dubious origin.

So, while Pliny's story may or may not be historically accurate, glass certainly had a beginning somewhere, and in the absence of

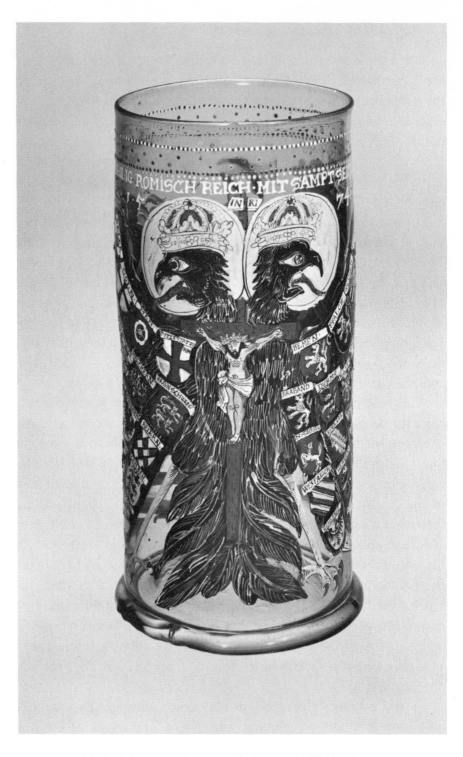

FIGURE 12. Reichsadler Humpen. Bohemia (1574). *Courtesy, The Corning Museum of Glass, Corning, N. Y.*

FIGURE 13. Stiegel-type tumblers, possibly made in U.S.A. as wedding present (c. 1772–1774). *Courtesy, The Corning Museum of Glass, Corning, N. Y.*

fact we may indulge in plausible fiction. Glass is with us now, and we can trace its history, with certain gaps, by the material evidence of glass objects treasured in our museums, until the evidence becomes scarce and finally disappears altogether. Then Pliny's story comes to our rescue—perhaps a myth, perhaps a historical fact.

The first real evidence of continuous glass production dates from what historians call the "New Kingdom in Egypt," 1580 to 1085 B.C. During this 500-year period, covering the Eighteenth, Nineteenth, and Twentieth Dynasties, small pieces of hollow ware of the

FIGURE 14. Austrian tumbler with medallion depicting six saints
(1794). *Courtesy, The Corning Museum of Glass, Corning, N. Y.*

FIGURE 15. German tumbler, decorated by Samuel Mohn with a view of Meissen (early 19th century). *Courtesy, The Corning Museum of Glass, Corning, N. Y.*

FIGURE 16. Transparent amber glass jug with mold-blown decoration and signature of Ennion under handle. Probably Sidon, Syria (c. first half of 1st century A.D.). *Courtesy, The Corning Museum of Glass, Corning, N. Y.*

FIGURE 17. The Paris Plate. Possibly Antioch, Syria (c. 250–350 A.D.). *Courtesy, The Corning Museum of Glass, Corning, N.Y.*

FIGURE 18. Blown pattern molded bottle of "eggplant" color with opaque white threads. Probably Syria (c. 2nd–4th century A.D.). *Courtesy, The Corning Museum of Glass, Corning, N.Y.*

FIGURE 19. Blown bowl of greenish glass with engraved, winged male figure and inscription III EZ HC HC. Syria (3rd–4th century A.D.). *Courtesy, The Corning Museum of Glass, Corning, N.Y.*

FIGURE. 20. Gold glass medallion with portraits of Saints Peter and Paul. Probably Rome (early 4th century A.D.). *Courtesy, The Corning Museum of Glass, Corning, N. Y.*

FIGURE 21. Cup in two layers of clear glass with gold leaf decoration in between. Parthian or Sassanian (2nd–4th century, A.D.).
Courtesy, The Corning Museum of Glass, Corning, N. Y.

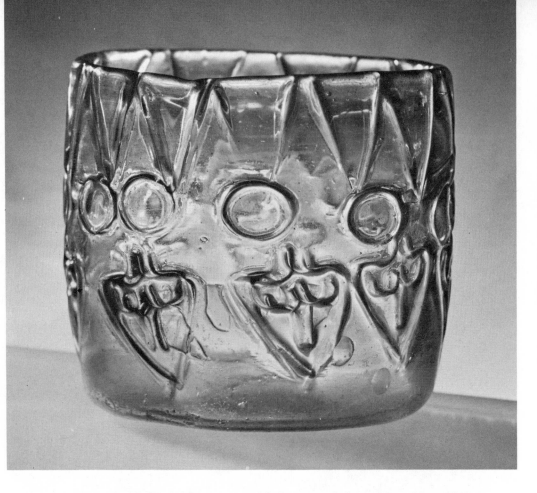

FIGURE 22. Free-blown cup with impressed decoration. Near East (8th–9th century A.D.). *Courtesy, The Corning Museum of Glass, Corning, N. Y.*

highest artistic quality were made by what is known as the "sand-core" method. Crude refractory material such as sand and clay was molded to the inside dimensions of the hollow piece to be made. This core was attached to the end of a copper rod and then submerged in molten glass and withdrawn. The thin layer of glass adhered to the core and was rolled smooth, perhaps on a slab of polished marble. Designs of colored glass thread (called "snake thread") were sometimes trailed around the piece and flattened into the wall by again rolling it on the marble. (See p.163) Sometimes the glass thread was left in bas-relief. Handles could then be added if desired.

48

FIGURE 23. Egyptian amphoriskos, probably a cosmetic container (c. 1450–1350 B.C.). *Courtesy, The Corning Museum of Glass, Corning, N. Y.*

FIGURE 24. Egyptian glass bottles (probably 6th century, B.C. and 6th–1st century, B.C.). *Courtesy, Victoria & Albert Museum, London, Crown Copyright.*

It appears that many of these small treasures were used by the great ladies surrounding the Pharaohs as containers for their scented oils and cosmetics, although it was not always possible to remove all of the sand core from the finished piece. A number of ruins of glass factories dating back to the New Kingdom have been discovered. The oldest of these, at Thebes, dates from the reign of Amenhotep III of the late Eighteenth Dynasty. Others at Tel el Amarna date from the reign of Akhnaton.

I left Leerdam completely fascinated by all I had seen, and obsessed with one question: How many of the techniques I had watched could be adapted to work, on a smaller scale, with the torch? During my training as a metallurgist I had already learned to make, and mend, delicate glass apparatus for the chemical laboratory.

I started to experiment at home, at first using an early type of burner that used city gas and forced air from a foot bellows. Some of the results were encouraging, but I soon grew tired of the continuous pumping of the foot bellows, which detracted from the steady actions of the hands. My next torch burned city gas, but oxygen took the place of the forced air. This produced a much hotter flame, and allowed me to concentrate all my attention on my hands. Bigger pieces of glass could now be worked. Since that time, through many years, I have used a great variety of torches to gain more refined control over my work.

No teachers were, or are, available for the kind of work that I wanted to do. Keeping clearly in mind what I had seen in Leerdam, and subsequently in other European centers of glassmaking, I had to evolve my own methods from the start. I carried on my private enterprise of experiment and research much in the manner of some of my professional work as a metallurgist—learning by trial and error just what I could expect to accomplish with my chosen materials and tools.

I felt no urge to go outside my home and set myself up with a

51

factory for the actual making of glass from its basic raw materials. Like the woodcarver who owns no forest of trees, and the artist in metals who is not concerned with the refining of the ore, I was, and still am, content to purchase my glass in the form of rods and tubes of various diameters. Forming glass, not making it from raw materials, was, and is still, my interest, since I wanted to evolve techniques that could be practiced in the average home. I taught myself to pigment glass, using various metallic oxides. I learned to respect the practical implications of such phrases as "softening point," "strain point," "annealing temperature," and "coefficient of expansion." I knew that natural laws govern the behavior of all substances, and that glass is no exception.

Nonetheless, there were innumerable failures. Molten glass on the end of a blowpipe in the free air is difficult to control, no matter how much theory one has learned. My growing scrapheap was my best teacher in those days. It has diminished in size through the years, but it is always with me as a reminder of my relative ignorance and imperfect mastery of technique.

Fortunately for my present pupils, they do not have to blaze the winding trail that I have followed. All the necessary steps for acquiring basic skills are clearly laid out for them in this book.

CHAPTER 3

Some Creative Philosophy

The island of Mallorca (or Majorca) is the largest of the Balearic Islands that belong to Spain. Sun-drenched, with typical limestone scenery, its magnificent sandy beaches are washed by the bluest of warm Mediterranean waters off the Costa Brava. It forms a triangle with Barcelona and Valencia, about 200 kilometers from each.

After strenuous weeks in the cold northern countries we flew from London to this alluring island to thaw out and to visit an ancient glass factory called Gordiola, which stands in the shadow of the cathedral in the capital city of Palma.

The glassmakers of Gordiola work with furnaces fired by wood, instead of the oil used in more modern factories. They produce good, inexpensive decorative pieces: vases, bowls, drinking glasses and the like, in great variety. Some of the workers are highly skilled. Half a dozen apprentice boys (Fig. 25) were dexterously forming green bulls on the end of pontils, for sale to visitors. Nothing in Palma is very far from the bull ring, which attracts great crowds to witness the barbaric performance. Green bulls are popular mementoes of this so-called sport. Certainly the activity of the corrida

FIGURE 25. Apprentices at Gordiola glass factory, Mallorca.

demands a kind of nimble, strenuous human effort not readily to be seen elsewhere in Palma in the more rational pursuits of trade.

But what happens to the visitors who fill the luxury hotels on the waterfront and spend their vacations eating, sleeping, sight-seeing, shopping, and sometimes even swimming in the friendly blue sea? Like similar visitors to all the Grand Palava hotels everywhere who believe they want nothing so much as to do nothing, relax, and be served from morning till night, they quickly become bored with the sameness of their unproductive routine and supposed luxury.

According to Sir Winston Churchill, men (and women) die from one of three main causes. They are either toiled, worried, or bored to death. Churchill announced this thought-provoking conclusion in his absorbing little book, *Painting as a Pastime*. If you haven't read it, you should.

54

He wastes no time on the problems of the unfortunates for whom life has become nothing but a bore. Only some stern discipline will help them. But for those who belong to the toiled and worried groups he offers solace and regeneration through creative hand work—especially painting.

"Take a joy ride in a paint box" was the advice he himself took at a time of intense worry and frustration. Worry is a spasm of the emotions. To fight it with one's will only gives it more strength. Some new and absorbing creative interest must be cunningly introduced to the attention of the worrier. The tight grip on the cause of worry will then begin to relax, and the tormenting spasm will disappear.

Painting came to Churchill's rescue at a critical moment in his meteoric career. Demoted from top leadership, he was obliged to be a powerless witness to a complete mishandling or abandonment of plans he had initiated. He knew nothing of painting, but, resolving to do it alone, he bought paints, brushes and oil. But how to start? He stood cowering in front of a snow-white canvas, smallest brush in hand, irresolute, and afraid to affront the white surface with even a tiny touch of blue. Then a friend, the wife of a great painter, dropped in to see him.

"Painting, eh! Well, what are you waiting for?" she cried. "Give me the brush—no, the big one!" She splashed into the oil, then the cerulean blue, then made bold sweeps across the upper part of the affronted canvas. The spell was broken. The canvas did not strike back. Sir Winston began his paint-box joy ride, and it wasn't too long before his pictures were exhibited in the Royal Academy.

Leaving it to the great masters to paint the great masterpieces, the untrained novice must have the audacity to make a start on his own. And what an adventure it may well turn out to be! What endless hours of absorbing pleasure—squeezing rich colors from the silver tubes, mixing, matching, comparing, studying light and shade, and building on the canvas the semblance of some treasured scene. Self-motivated and self-taught activity such as this will dispel worry from the mind and take the furrow of anxiety from the brow. If I owned a Grand Palava hotel, I would equip every room with a paint box, and hang the walls with the paintings executed by former visitors.

Kipling advised digging in the garden to banish care and to return the mind to healthy functioning. "Dig till you gently perspire, and then you will find the sun and the wind, and the djinn of the garden too, has lifted the hump, the horrible hump, the hump that is black and blue."

My own experience is that a measure of travel for travel's sake, with no other purpose in mind but to change the scene, be entertained, served, and idle, certainly has its place. But it quickly begins to pall. I find I must travel with a creative purpose that runs through all the adventures of the road like the string through a necklace of beads. To most people, perhaps, work is work and pleasure is pleasure. They try to combine a minimum of work with a maximum of pleasure, and who can blame them? I believe I am most fortunate in that my chosen work is also my greatest pleasure, and I can never find hours enough to accomplish all that I want to do.

A dear friend of mine, the late Amelita Galli-Curci, was generally considered to be one of the greatest coloraturas of all time, yet she never had one singing lesson. She just opened her mouth and sang like a bird. Of course she had something to sing about, so she sang it with all that she had. In opera and concert for over 40 years, she delighted audiences around the world, and, like the bird, never looked back for the applause that was lavished on her.

"If you can talk, then you can sing," she used to tell me. "Sing, then, if you feel the urge. Sing the simplest notes—never strain after effect—discover your own capacity. Work with it, and you'll find it grows and grows. Don't bother about taking lessons. Just sing in the open air to the woods and lakes and mountains. Sing for joy and for sorrow if you must—they are both parts of life. Improvise, compose while you sing, don't limit yourself to the compositions of others. Be yourself in song. It is as natural as breathing or talking."

Galli-Curci did just that, and she enthralled the world. Later in life she underwent a thyroid operation and could sing no more in public. What did she do but take up oil painting! Without instruction, but with the audacity of the creative experimenter, she turned the rich temperament of the natural singer to another colorful art, and once more she triumphed. Her voice is now still, but she lives on in memory—the self-taught Italian songbird who sang, as later she painted, for the sheer joy of it.

Most of us, unfortunately, are taught very early in life to think of ourselves in a very confining way. A few of our abilities are praised and rewarded, while most of our potential remains ignored and often denied by our elders. So we become convinced about the things we can and cannot do, and too often come to regard ourselves as nothing more than a kind of aggregate of the things we can do. We then stress too much our accredited achievements that result from our specialist's training, and too little the undiscovered or unexercised potential of our multi-faceted nature. Yet maturing individuals often find themselves excelling at the very things they were told in school they were not fitted for. It is said that Albert Einstein's teachers prophesied that he would never amount to anything. It is the audacious attempt to achieve something in which we have had no training that really claims our interest. In making the attempt we learn the kind of independent self-confidence that is the birthright of every free individual.

Our own intimate feelings and desires are continually generating new forms within our minds. These become clearly defined as we brood over them, gradually emerging from the subtle and invisible to clothe themselves with objective reality. This is an experience common to us all—from emotion to thought, and finally into dynamic action in the visible world. That is the creative process continually at work in every one of us.

Nature surrounds us with one stupendous work of art, not of

our making, but ever changing, ever renewed before our eyes. Shall we who claim to be nature's supreme masterpiece of creation not accept and give rein to our own many-faceted creative nature? The single label we commonly hang on ourselves and on our friends—doctor, lawyer, or whatever—represents only a part of us. There is more to the man than what he learned in school, and now uses to serve society and earn a living. Important as that work may be, it does not exhaust his potential. It is one facet of himself that he has taken the trouble to polish highly, and which he has come to be known by. It is his *carte de visite,* his passport, certified by competent authority, and guarantees status and respect from his fellows in addition to his daily bread.

If he is wise, part of his leisure hours will be spent alone in a private oasis of his own making, where he may exercise creative talents other than those used in the performance of his professional work. In that oasis he may embark, with audacity, on any creative adventure that attracts him and is consistent with the welfare of his neighbors.

I have a friend, a great surgeon, who spends two hours every Sunday morning washing the windows of his house. Some people probably think him strange. Why should a surgeon waste his time washing windows? But he is not wasting time. He can't spend his whole life in surgery. He has staked his skill all week long on saving lives in the operating room. Now he must claim some time to be alone with himself. His window washing occupies his senses with exercise devoid of all anxiety, and acts as an excluding agent against all intrusions. He always comes in for lunch refreshed and vital; the windows now shine and sparkle, and let in all the light, and may even, from force of habit, have been sterilized! My friend may never be as famous for his clean windows as for his surgery, but in his case the two things are complementary, and he gives all he has to each in turn. As for myself, I always love to see anyone working with glass!

"Keep up with, circle round and round your life, as a dog does his master's chaise," wrote Thoreau. "Do what you love. Know your own bone: gnaw at it, bury it, unearth it, and gnaw it still. Be good for something. Let nothing come between you and the light." Not even a dirty window! My doctor friend really gnaws on his bone—surgery at one end, window washing at the other—and it's the same bone.

A well-rounded, highly diversified life is every man's dream for himself, or ought to be. The hazards and beauties of the road he tramps are about the same for all. The difference lies in the traveler. Is he his own friend? Has he discovered and nurtured resources that make him a match for all occasions? Does he travel always seeking escape from a haunting fear of what might be around the next corner?

In Switzerland I heard the story of two mountaineers who became enveloped by clouds and lost sight of one another in the high Alps. The first man to reach the summit waited anxiously for his friend who finally arrived out of breath and half scared out of his wits. He said that a huge giant had followed him up the mountain, and that, in a frantic effort to escape, he had fallen and sprained his ankle.

"A giant—what kind of giant?" his friend inquired.

"I never actually caught sight of him, but his shadow kept appearing on the clouds. He marched up behind me all the way!"

"A giant like that followed me too," replied the first man. "It was my shadow!"

Too many of us know too little about ourselves as we tramp and climb the common road, pursued by the menacing shadow of our unfulfilled lives.

CHAPTER 4

Venice and Glass

More than a hundred years ago Turner, the great English painter, gave us a word picture of Venice. "A city of rose and white, rising out of an emerald sea against a sky of sapphire blue." Turner's masterpieces in oil speak still more eloquently of what seems to be a floating dream of color and form rather than an inhabited city— a marriage of rose-pearl clouds, iridescent waters, and the graceful lines of Byzantine palaces.

After arriving in the bustle and hurry of the railroad station, a haunting tranquillity begins to invade the mind as one floats through the twilight of a summer evening in a gondola along the narrow waterways to a hotel on the Grand Canal. In the ancient part of Venice, with its innumerable canals and stately bridges, little has changed since Turner knew it, and the sun goes down behind the dome of Saint Mark's as it has done for nearly a thousand years.

Venice and glass . . . glass and Venice! The two seem inseparable, and no wonder. What but glass, graceful in form and wedded to the rainbow, the very chalice for light and color, could serve to capture for the Venetian artists the translucent qualities of their

FIGURE 26. Venetian plate (1513–1534). *Courtesy, The Corning Museum of Glass, Corning, N. Y.*

FIGURE 28. Venetian salver, free-blown with applied and tooled decoration and diamond-scratched engraving (end, 17th century). *Courtesy, The Corning Museum of Glass, Corning, N. Y.*

environment? Long before those giants among Venetian painters, Titian and Tintoretto, died in the sixteenth century, the glass art had found its way to Venice and was firmly established there. The *Museo Vitrario di Murano* is a place of both delight and bewilderment. The seemingly endless variety of glass creations from the hands of artists long dead always arouses deep emotion in me. Delight comes first from sharing so lavish a feast of beauty, then bewilderment from insufficient knowledge on my part of the men and the times in which they worked. I am not an historian of glass. Only

FIGURE 27. Candlestick of latticinio glass. Façon de Venise (early 17th century). *Courtesy, The Corning Museum of Glass, Corning, N. Y.*

63

FIGURE 29. Functional and ornamental glasswork from the Museo e Gallerie Nazionali di Capodimonte, Naples, Italy.

FIGURE 30. Functional and ornamental glasswork from the Museo e Gallerie Nazionali di Capodimonte, Naples, Italy.

FIGURE 31. Glass chandelier from the Museo e Gallerie Nazionali di Capodimonte, Naples, Italy.

FIGURE 32. Venetian goblet with cover (end, 15th century). *Courtesy, Victoria & Albert Museum, London, Crown Copyright.*

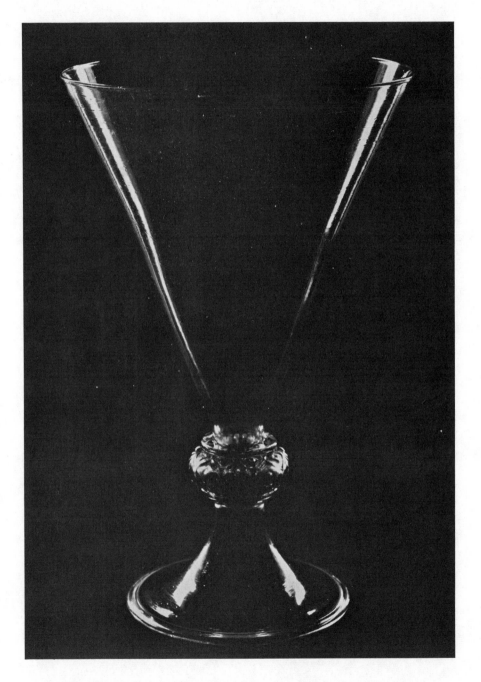

FIGURE 33. Italian or French goblet (second half, 16th century). *Courtesy, Victoria & Albert Museum, London, Crown Copyright.*

as an appreciator of quality, design, color, and technical skill can I render homage to the past. The often uncertain attempt to fix names and dates and historical influences I must leave to those whose painstaking research qualifies them to announce facts.

After a couple of hours spent in musing over favorite pieces, I find myself turning from the past to the present, and longing either to be at work in my own studio or watching what other living creators are doing in the here and now. My own workshop being in California, thousands of miles away, I go to visit my friends at the factory of Barovier and Toso on the island of Murano.

But why this particular factory? Let me explain by recounting very briefly some interesting history. About the time of the conquest of Egypt by the Romans, the whole of the Eastern Mediterranean was a hotbed of glassmaking activity, Tyre and Sidon being the principal centers from the first century B.C. to the first century A.D. Naturally, the knowledge of glassmaking was brought to Italy and spread through all the lands dominated by Rome. After the fall of the Roman Empire, the glass art industry suffered a severe decline and was all but lost for a period of nearly 600 years. The Middle Ages saw groups of glassworkers coming together to lay the foundations of a new industry, this time in Venice. The enterprise flourished, and, as the fame of Venetian glass became widespread, its importance as an economic factor in the life of a wealthy and powerful community led the authorities to take drastic measures to ensure that the secrets of the workers should not be stolen or shared by foreigners. As early as 1291, the glass furnaces were ordered removed from Venice to the small island of Murano, about two miles away. The glassworkers were ordered to live on the island and leave it only by special permission, under penalty of heavy fines and even death should they disobey. The year 1350 saw

FIGURE 34. Venetian bouquetier (17th century). *Courtesy, Victoria & Albert Museum, London, Crown Copyright.*

the beginning of a veritable dynasty of glassmakers, the Baroviers. Through the centuries, this family has produced creative artists of the highest attainment, contributing consistently through a period of 600 years to the preeminence of Venetian styles and workmanship, through what has been called the Second Golden Age of Glass.

The present Ercole Barovier inherited the firm "Artisti Barovier" from his father after World War I. In 1936 he founded a new factory, "Barovier & Toso." The brothers Artemio and Decio Toso also trace their glass tradition back to the seventeenth century. Today, Ercole Barovier, after 40 years of service, is still the chief designer and chemist of his firm. His son Angelo is a talented painter and glass designer. Father and son are seen in Figs. 35 and 36 as I photographed them in their factory. Figures 37 and 38 show pieces in the private Barovier Museum, all designed by Ercole Barovier, and representing work in progress in the factory.

FIGURE 35. Ercole and Angelo Barovier

FIGURE 36. Fluted piece of hollow ware being made at the Barovier
& Toso glass factory.

FIGURE 37. Glass pieces designed by Ercole Barovier.

FIGURE 38. Glass pieces designed by Ercole Barovier.

CHAPTER 5

When You Play with Glass…

"When you play with glass, does it ever come out an animal?"

I was arranging my equipment for a lecture-demonstration in a museum, and this very special question came from a bright-eyed, eager little girl teetering on one foot beside my workbench. At the tender age of seven or eight she quite naturally assumed that I was "playing," and that the glass was free to be as capricious as a fairy and choose its role in the game. It might "come out" that I should find myself playing with an animal, just because the glass felt like that at the time. My part was to help it. At all events, the play is the thing, and the living glass should be free to unfold its own character —perhaps its animal nature.

There were many other questions that afternoon, and although they were voiced by children, they came really from the adults who had prematurely withered childish fancy with unimaginative grown-up talk and behavior. They were all grown-up questions, and they did not light up the young faces of the questioners with eagerness as they asked them. Not one of these questions lodges in my memory. But talking with this little girl perched on one foot was a delight. She fully understood what I often find myself trying to explain to grown-up audiences.

The most frequent question I get after a lecture-demonstration is this: "Do you know exactly what you are going to make before you start to work?" I suppose it is a good question, and my answer always runs something like this: Yes, quite often I have decided beforehand just what I shall make, and I follow through with the plan to the end. But very frequently I change horses in mid-stream, and end up at some entirely unexpected place on the opposite bank —often, if not always, a much more interesting place than the one I had planned to reach before entering the flow of action. It is while engaged in the creative act itself, not in the mental plan for creative activity, that imaginative feeling takes over the helm. The journey is the reality, not the tickets and maps and guidebooks, nor even the anticipated destination. Free passage, made possible by technical skills that have become second nature, is what the imagination demands as the condition for its full release.

Naturally, if you must build a steel bridge over a river, a competent engineer had better make the plan, and his plan had better be carried out to the letter. The prime function of such a bridge is its utility, which is not to say that it may not be beautiful as well. But the principal considerations in designing the bridge are the cold hard facts of stresses and strains and mathematical calculations. If, on the other hand, the bridge you want to build is to span the gulf between the desperate, news-shocked mind of a modern adult and the enchanted land he once inhabited as a starry-eyed child, then by all means let the right child be your engineer and your guide on the farther shore. More than arms to defend, and bombs to destroy, we need to learn from our children that life is meant to be lived gloriously, creatively, playfully—not despoiled and dissipated in toil that brings no happiness, and strife that brings only misery and death. The Irish poet, George Russell ("A.E."), wrote a memorable line: "In the lost boyhood of Judas, Christ was betrayed."

Thank heaven for little girls and little boys, and thank heaven for those grown-ups whose living has led them to recapture the unimpaired vision of the loved and healthy child that turns the world into his garden and all living things into his friends.

"Does it ever come out an animal?" That phrase caught me, as I love to be caught, in an un-grown-up moment in which memories of my own happy childhood welled up in response to the little child at my side.

According to an ancient legend, "today" and "tomorrow" don't quite fit together. For just a split second, as the clock strikes the last stroke of midnight, a dazzling light shines through a narrow crack. Algernon Blackwood, the distinguished writer, wove a charming story around this legend in his book called *The Education of Uncle Paul*. Children everywhere have always been able to squeeze through this crack to the land where dreams are realities, where all broken toys are mended, where everything loved and lost is found. The little brother who suddenly "went away" after he had been in bed with the fever—he is there, and so is Rover the spaniel, who was run over by an automobile.

If grown-ups can be caught in an un-grown-up moment by a child who gives the command: "As you really are!", they, too, can throw all their troubles away and squeeze through the crack with their children. For most of us it takes a child to remove the self-protective and often pretentious masks we habitually wear and give us back to ourselves whole, simple and playful.

While exploring a tide-water pool on the beach, I once spotted a small hermit crab. Half in and half out of his cumbersome borrowed shell, he was toiling along the sandy bottom searching for food. I picked him out of the cool water and placed him on my open palm. This was a new and bewildering experience for the crab. After dragging his heavy shelter around my warm hand, he suddenly threw all caution to the wind and ran right out into the open. His soft body had been deformed by the protective, confining shell, but there he was free, facing the unknown, and completely vulnerable. Not wanting to frighten him out of his own skin as well, I dropped him back into the pool and placed his old shell house beside him. I watched and waited, hoping to witness the process of reentry. But it did not happen. Perhaps it felt good to be free! I am not a hermit crab, so I can't be sure. Perhaps he went back to his old protective armor after I had wandered on. All I know is that it did "come out" an animal, though I was not playing with glass!

In my hand I hold a tube of plastic cement, the kind that dries clear as ice. I use it to mend broken glass. After use, the tube is closed by inserting a pin into the tiny hole through which the material is squeezed out in a thin thread. The pin is encrusted with dried plastic at the end farthest from its point. Inside the tube all is liquid. It has never been exposed to the drying air. As yet it remains uncommitted to fulfilling any function, performing any task—a reservoir untapped. Once squeezed through the tiny opening at the end of the tube, it is committed—perhaps usefully, perhaps wastefully. It hardens in whatever position and shape it assumes. So it exists until disintegrated through time or accident—immobilized and static.

We are not machines, designed and made to fulfill only a series of preordained, comformist tasks, but creative creatures, capable of the most astonishing new adventures. Much, if not most, of our motivation is irrational and unpredictable even to ourselves, so that, when we take hold of any substance to make our imprint upon it, the results may be wholly unexpected. We may find ourselves attending the birth of an unpremeditated offspring. Certain men are continually breaking away from traditional paths to blaze new trails.

When technique serves only to release a true creative talent, the flow of action seems effortless and natural. Technique by itself has nothing to communicate except the fact that he who uses it has found nothing of his own to say. Why linger over your past creations? Each new day brings fresh inspiration for unique achievement. Go about the business of your own creation, unmoved by the praise or censure of the crowd.

CHAPTER **6**

Famous Glasshouses

Eighteenth-century glassworkers in northern Europe enjoyed many privileges not commonly the lot of their neighbors and friends. Glass was a relatively scarce commodity, and perhaps that fact allowed the masters of the art to write their own tickets with the owners of the factories. At any rate, we are told in the history of Kosta, Sweden's oldest glassworks founded in 1742, and originally owned by the Crown, that the workers' contracts guaranteed them two rooms, a kitchen, and the services of a maid. This was something very far from common at that period. The heat from the furnaces apparently evoked tremendous thirst in the men as they worked at their tasks, for free beer—up to four gallons a shift per man—was also assured!

If glassblowers attended a party, all other guests had to wear their Sunday-best clothes, and no one was permitted to address the glass men by their first names. During the cold weather the warm, light workshops were popular meeting places for young and old. They fried herring and potatoes at the furnaces, drank and swapped stories, and often the strains of the accordion were heard. Even the glass salesmen, often aged and retired glassworkers, were banded

FIGURE 39. Early master's bench at Kosta glass works, Sweden.

into a group proud of its special standing in the community. They wandered the roads with ox carts filled with glass packed in straw and fern leaves to make their sales.

We made several trips into the beautiful forests of Småland, about 50 kilometers from Kalmar, to visit the leading Swedish glass factories of Kosta and Orrefors, located in the forest for the sake of cheap wood fuel for the factories.

The name Kosta combines the first syllables of the names of its two founders—General Anders *Ko*skull and General Georg Bogislaus *Sta*el von Holsten, governors of the counties of Kronoberg and Kalmar. Both of these gentlemen had helped Charles XII to defeat Peter the Great at Narva. A cousin of Stael von Holsten was Swedish Minister to France, while his wife, as "Madame de Stael," was one of the best-known writers of the Napoleonic era.

The practical work of making glass was begun by four glass-blowers imported from Germany, then the leading glass-producing nation. The chief product was small greenish-tinted window panes—the so-called "moon glass" featuring the "bull's eye" where the blowpipe had been removed (Figs. 40 and 41). Within two years 12 cases of these panes went into the building of the Royal Palace in Stockholm for King Frederik I. Then followed glass chandeliers, which were soon in demand for churches and the houses of the aristocracy. Lowly beer tumblers and akvavit glasses and sugar shakers were produced for inns in Småland and were in demand by the nobles and the Court.

The year 1839 saw the installation of mechanical production for pressed glass. Plates, sugar bowls, cream pitchers, and a variety

FIGURE 40. "Bull's eye" glass at Stourbridge, England (1794).

FIGURE 41. "Bull's eye" glass door at Stourbridge, England.

FIGURE 42. Kosta glass.

of household wares quickly found their way into the humblest cottages. Then exports began, and trade spread to England, the United States, Russia, and far-away India. Kosta's famous "Ducat Bowls" date from this period. These were of heavy crystal, elaborately cut with deep grooves to cause intense play of light. One magnificent example was bought for the collection of the Czar of Russia.

The twentieth century saw a swing to purely Swedish design, led by Axel Hummel, then manager of Kosta, who hired the painter Gunnar Wennerber to produce more artistic and imaginative designs. Today, Vicke Lindstrand is his modern successor, and has earned a well-deserved reputation for original work of the highest quality.

FIGURE 43. Kosta glass.

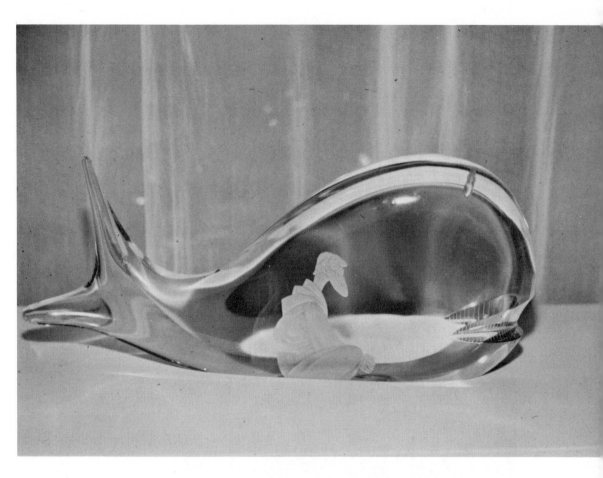

FIGURE 44. Kosta glass whale.

FIGURE 45. Glory hole at Orrefors factory, Sweden.

FIGURE 46. Form molding at Orrefors factory, Sweden.

FIGURE 47. Orrefors glasses.

FIGURE 48. Orrefors glassware.

FIGURE 49. Orrefors vases.

FIGURE 50. Orrefors goblet and compote.

FIGURE 51. Orrefors ornamental glass.

FIGURE 52. Orrefors pieces.

CHAPTER 7

Adventures in Holland, England, and Denmark

Two branches of the river Rhine meet in the center of the pictur-esque old town of Leyden, about 10 miles from The Hague in south Holland. Rembrandt was born in Leyden in 1606 and painted some of his masterpieces there between 1627 and 1631. One of Europe's oldest and most renowned universities was founded in 1575 by William of Orange, and has stood on the an-cient site of the Convent of White Nuns, near the center of the town, since 1581.

The Museum of Antiquities is a part of the university, and it was there that we attended a conference called "International Glass Days"—five of them—rubbing shoulders with glass historians, scholars and experts, collectors, and directors of the great museums from all over the world. We listened to lectures, with two language translations coming through earphones, and took part in confer-ences. In between times we visited other public and private collec-tions of glass. It was a rich experience. The conference had been organized by the very energetic and competent Dr. Joseph Philippe, Director of the Musée du Verre in Liège, Belgium, where, I am

FIGURE 54. Diamond-stipple engraved goblet, signed "F. Greenwood."
England and Netherlands (1746). *Courtesy, The Corning Museum of
Glass, Corning, N. Y.*

FIGURE 53. Engraved *roemer*. Nether-
lands (17th century). *Courtesy, The
Corning Museum of Glass, Corning,
N. Y.*

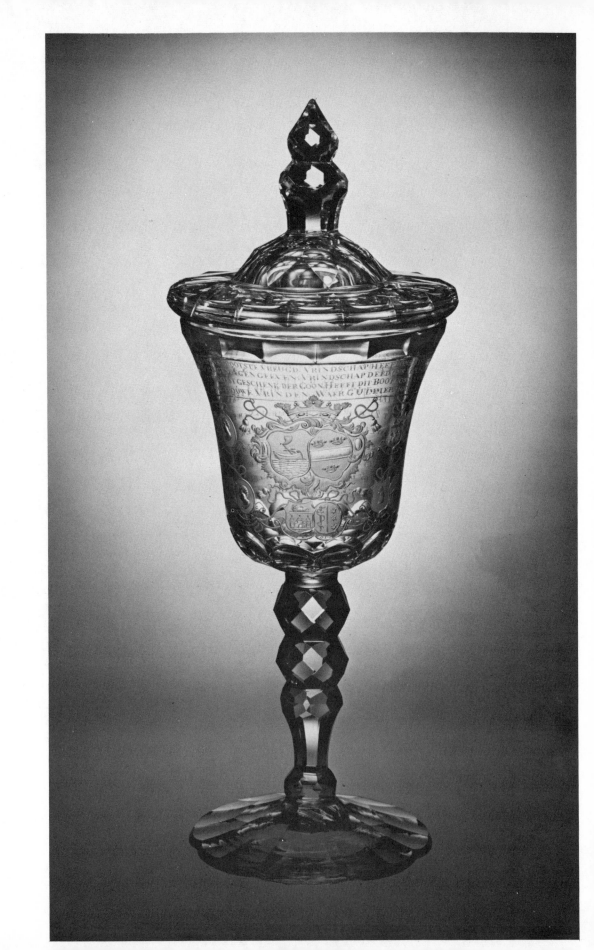

proud to say, a group of my own pieces has since found its way into the permanent collection.

The lectures and discussions were all recorded and printed in book form. They make fascinating reading, for they underscore the continuous painstaking efforts of expert researchers to complete and enrich the long romantic history of glass, and to extol the people responsible for its innumerable phases. I believe that copies of the book may be obtained from the Musée du Verre, Liège, Belgium.

One paper held out the hope that the shapes of miniature glass pieces in a famous Dutch doll's house of known date might provide accurate help in dating and placing normal-sized pieces of similar shape. Similar help might be given by famous paintings of the Dutch masters containing glass pieces, and known to have been executed in certain years.

My wife took special pleasure in the magnificent collection of glass beads from all over the world, lent by Dr. W. G. N. van der Sleen. If I could copy certain specimens from Zanzibar, she would be willing to buy clothes to match them! I do make beads for her, but no copies. It is always the accessories that cost the most!

Visits to once familiar places are always tinged with sadness when familiar faces are no longer there. Leerdam re-visited was no exception, though we were welcomed most warmly by the present management. The Cochius house where I had once enjoyed the hospitality of my friends is now a national glass museum. The exterior of the house looks just as I remembered it; even the interior structure is not much changed. But when we walked upstairs to what was once my bedroom, we found it lined with exhibition cases filled with prized glass pieces from the hands of a Dutch artist,

FIGURE 55. Free-blown, cut and engraved, covered goblet of clear, heavy glass, decorated with a pair of coats-of-arms on bowl, with a royal crown above, and framed by five pairs of coats-of-arms with inscriptions. On the pontil mark in diamond point appears "J. Sang 1769." The Netherlands. *Courtesy, The Corning Museum of Glass, Corning, N. Y.*

FIGURE 57. Reverse painting on glass, copied from an original of George Washington by Gilbert Stuart. Chinese (c. 1798–1800). *Courtesy, The Corning Museum of Glass, Corning, N. Y.*

FIGURE 56. Translucent white glass goblet. Façon de Venise, probably Liège. *Courtesy, The Corning Museum of Glass, Corning, N. Y.*

Mr. F. Maydam, who is carving out a wonderful career for himself. While we were busy inspecting everything, strange music began floating up from the ground floor. It turned out to be a German recording of an instrument made of glass. You may, at some dinner party, have made a kind of music by circular motions of a wet finger on the thin rim of a champagne glass. This sound had something of the same quality—pure tone, yet somewhat shrill. It came from a glass harp, constructed by Bruno Hoffmann between 1929 and 1935, consisting of a series of glass bowls set in wood to ensure proper resonance. The bowls, which vary in size, are played with wet fingertips like the champagne glass. But there the analogy ends, for we were hearing compositions by Mozart and Beethoven, played on a harp that has three and a half octaves (chromatic).

Perhaps you may recall that in 1762 Benjamin Franklin invented what he called a glass armonica. This consisted of a series of glass bowls of diminishing size, mounted one inside the other on a horizontal rotating shaft. Nimble, wet fingertips were used to bring the instrument to life and render music specially written by Mozart. Glass, you see, has a unique voice, and can be persuaded to charm our ears as well as delight our eyes. The whole story of Franklin's armonica can be found in a pamphlet by E. Power Biggs that is probably available at the Isabella Stewart Gardner Museum in Boston, Massachusetts.

Designs for decorative glass pieces, including tableware, have changed greatly since my first visit to Leerdam. Vividly colored pieces that find their way into streamlined modern dwellings and commercial buildings now fill the well-lighted showrooms, creating the momentary illusion of being in sunny Italy. Actually, outside the rain was falling steadily from a leaden sky, as it had done during most of July throughout Holland. Interiors enlivened by highly colored decor are much needed, especially in the low-key climates of the low countries. If variety is the spice of life, there is plenty of spice to be found in the showrooms at Leerdam, but not always in the Dutch weather.

98

FIGURE 58. Medallion portrait, signed "D. Bimann." Bohemia (1834). *Courtesy, The Corning Museum of Glass, Corning, N. Y.*

In his excellent book, *From Broad-Glass to Cut Crystal* (Leonard Hill Books, Ltd., London)—a history of the Stourbridge glass industry—D. R. Guttery tells us that in 1696 there were 88 glasshouses at work in England and Wales. Seventeen of these were located around the small town of Stourbridge, in Worcestershire, where glass has been made ever since. In 1709, needing a constant supply of good clay for the making of their melting pots, the glassworkers leased some clay pits from Lord Ward Dudley. The annual rent was one hundred pounds and 125 quarts of top-quality wine in bottles, to be delivered on December 25th at The Talbott Inn in Stourbridge.

We stayed at this same half-timbered, 500-year-old Talbot Inn (present spelling) while visiting the Foley College of Further Education, the only art school I know that offers practical courses in the traditional methods of offhand glass work. Kenneth S. Wainwright, who does the teaching, comes of a long line of glass masters who have worked in Stourbridge. His skill does credit to the family.

While "glass design" is taught in several famous British art schools, the students are offered no instruction in the practical art of glassmaking. So it is that Mr. Wainwright receives student drawings to be translated into three-dimensional reality. However, many of the dreams committed to paper by the aspiring designers cannot be made in glass at all. This places Mr. Wainwright in a dilemma with which I am quite familiar, since friends of mine frequently ask me to make outlandish objects that may rightly fit into their imagination, but not into glass. Of course, anyone who watches a pair of skilled hands dexterously manipulating hot viscous glass may understandably conclude that almost anything of

FIGURE 59. German or Dutch *roemer* (mid-17th century). *Courtesy, Victoria & Albert Museum, London, Crown Copyright.*

FIGURE 60. Exercise in scientific glass—Leerdam.

FIGURE 61.

FIGURE 62.

FIGURE 63.

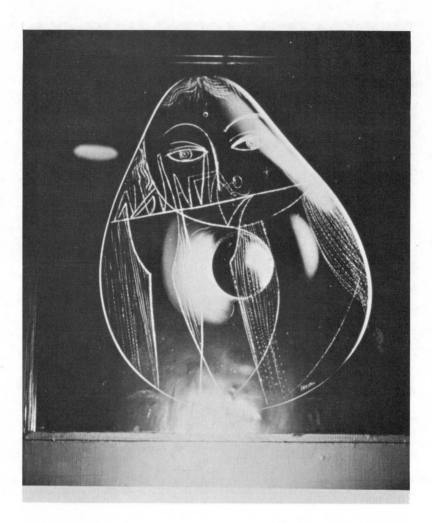

FIGURE 64.

FIGURE 65.

FIGURE 66.

reasonable size can be made from it. Certainly a master like Mr. Wainwright might be expected to perform miracles! But there are limits to the delicate elaboration of pieces that must afterward be annealed to prevent cracking. It is here that the dangers of sagging (drooping or collapsing under the influence of heat and gravity) any whispy threads, or other light ornamentations, that may have been fused to some more substantial object must give the practical craftsman pause. It is not always the problem of forming an intricate piece that determines what can and what cannot be made with success.

I brought a not unreasonable request to Mr. Wainwright. I wanted him to make a millefiori paperweight, and a goblet with an air-twist stem. On viewing such pieces in museums, the layman is generally completely baffled in his attempt to visualize the processes by which such pieces come into being. Descriptions are almost impossible without pictures. Mr. Wainwright readily agreed to my proposition, so I brought movie and still camera equipment to his workshop. Naturally, only the movie camera captured all that we saw, but Figs. 71–79 illustrate some of the steps.

FIGURE 67. Lead glass goblet from the Savoy Glasshouse of George Ravenscroft, London (c. 1676–1678). *Courtesy, The Corning Museum of Glass, Corning, N. Y.*

FIGURE 69. Free-blown bowl of light green glass with an opaque white rim. Engraved with a stag hunt, a drinking party, and a manor house bearing the arms of the Fitzwilliam and Walpole families. England (c. 1760). *Courtesy, The Corning Museum of Glass, Corning, N. Y.*

FIGURE 70. Puce glass plaque with white cameo-cut scene showing Venus and Cupid in a classical landscape, signed "George Woodall." England, Thomas Webb and Sons (c. 1890). *Courtesy, The Corning Museum of Glass, Corning, N.Y.*

FIGURE 71.

FIGURE 72.

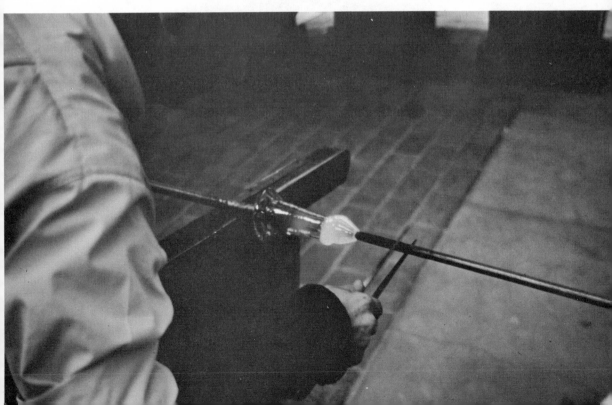

FIGURE 73.

FIGURE 74.

FIGURE 75.

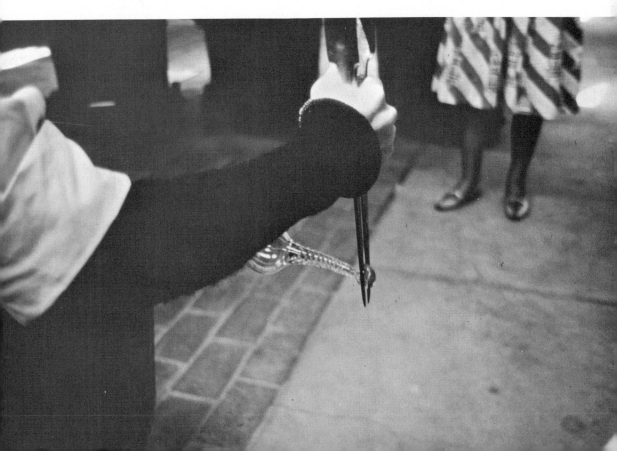

FIGURE 76.

FIGURE 77.

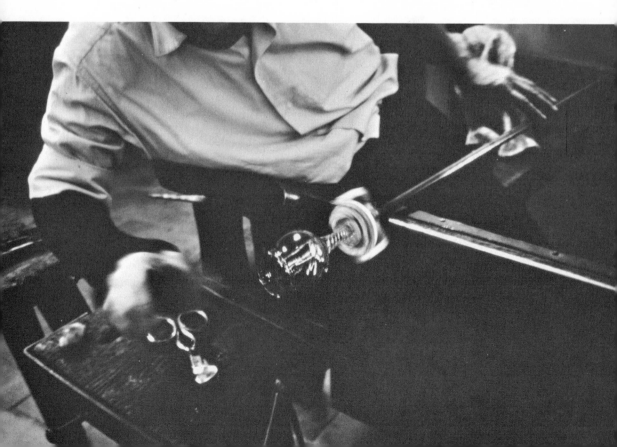

FIGURE 78.

FIGURE 79.

FIGURE 80. Pontils and blowpipes, Stourbridge, England.

THE AIR-TWIST GOBLET

A blob of molten glass (called a "gather") is gathered from the crucible in the furnace on the end of a four-foot blowing iron. The gather is marvered * to correct shape, and then blown into a bubble that will become the bowl of the goblet. Now another gather is marvered to correct shape, attached to the bubble at the point farthest from the blowpipe, and then pressed against four metal spikes to indent deep air pockets. These air pockets are now fire-sealed and the piece is elongated by twisting. This draws the air pockets into thin spirals. Another gather is attached to the stem, and tooled to form the foot of the goblet. The foot is now held in a special clamp on the end of a metal rod (called a "pontil"— see Fig. 80). The bubble is cracked from the blowpipe and tooled to form the desired shape of the bowl and the smooth rim. The finished piece is now placed in the annealing furnace, heated to a determined temperature below the softening point, and then cooled very slowly.

Note that Mr. Wainwright is using a girl student as his assistant. This was the first time I ever saw a woman engaged in factory-type offhand glass work. I see no reason why women should not excel in this as in any other art-craft.

THE MILLEFIORI PAPERWEIGHT

This was made in the following manner. Short lengths of colored glass rod are packed vertically, in a desired pattern, inside a stout, shallow metal mold. Now a marvered gather of clear glass on the end of a pontil is pressed into the mold to pick up the colored rods. A second gather of clear glass is made over the colored rods, trapping them in its center. Further re-heating, spinning, and shaping

* To "marver" is to roll heat-softened glass on the marver. The marver used in large factories is a flat polished steel surface. The marver in the context of this book is the carbon flat (see Fig. 90).

120

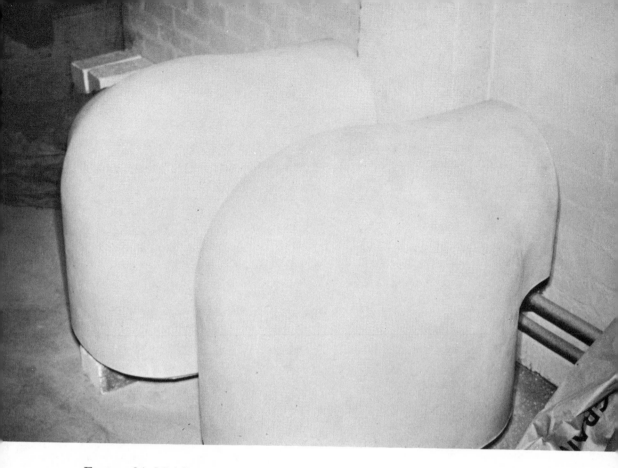

FIGURE 81. Melting pots, Stourbridge, England.

FIGURE 82.

Figure 83.

FIGURE 84.

FIGURE 85.

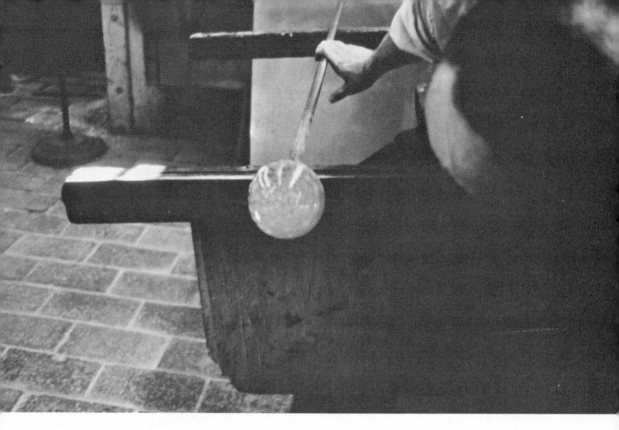

FIGURE 86.

FIGURE 87.

FIGURE 88.

at the master's chair produces the finished piece. This is cracked from the pontil by a drop of water, and annealed.

Back at the Talbot Inn, I took pictures of rare examples of "bull's eye" or "moon glass," dating from about 1790 (see Figs. 40, 41).

When summer comes to Denmark, the whole countryside wakes gratefully from its pall of short gloomy days and displays a startling feast of green and color. Lilacs, laburnum and hawthorn—not just isolated trees, but long hedges of them—spring into vivid bloom against a unique blue sky, the kind of blue that has inspired the artists of Danish porcelain for centuries.

One morning we paid homage to the Little Mermaid perched on her rock looking across the harbor of Copenhagen—or København, as the Danes write it—which means the "merchant's port." We drove down the Langelinie and on to the beautiful highway that runs along the edge of the sound through woods of beech and elm, and old villages with their country villas, all the 40 kilometers to Hamlet's Castle at Helsingör.

My wife, whose family on the distaff side has lived in Denmark since 1700, knows every inch of the road. She recalled the names of places, relatives, and friends she had loved so much in her youth. Suddenly we arrived at Humlebeck, the main object of our morning's ride, and turned off the main road to find the new modern museum called Louisiana. Nestled among woods, and stretching across broad lawns on the edge of the sound that separates Denmark from Sweden, Louisiana fulfills completely my own idea of what a museum for moderns should be. Architects Jorgen Bo and Vilhelm Wohlert have blended their exciting modern structures with those of a stately mansion built more than a hundred years ago by a Danish nobleman who had had three wives, each named Louise—hence Louisiana!

The visitor discovers dramatic glimpses of pools, magnificent shade trees, and a far view of blue water and the coast of Sweden, as he wanders through galleries of tastefully mounted exhibits—a re-

FIGURE 89. sculpture in the Louisiana Museum, Denmark.

freshing blend of the man-made with the indulgent smiling face of nature. As Knud W. Jensen, the director, has said, "There is a holiday mood here in which everything seems fresh and new. In congenial surroundings the interplay of the various arts should be obvious and natural. Architecture, landscape gardening, painting, sculpture, graphic arts and handicrafts—all belong to each other, and are all expressions of the time in which we live. Each single artist contributes toward developing our concept of reality, as he creates something beautiful and true that has not existed before. One cannot help being delighted and thankful that art exists in a world otherwise full of destructive forces." Never visit Denmark without spending a day at Louisiana.

In Denmark we have many friends. Two of these are the gentlemanly skorstenfejer (silk-hatted chimneysweeps) we met outside the king's summer palace, begrimed from hat to foot with soot from the royal chimneys. Then there are, or were, several storks that we found nesting on the roof of an old cottage. We didn't actually talk with the storks, but they must have befriended us. In Denmark, for hundreds of years, meeting with skorstenfejer or sighting storks has been a sure sign of coming luck. Our luck came in this way. I had given a list of rare books on glass to a well-known antiquarian and a similar list to an ordinary bookstore, with requests that they search for copies. So far on our travels we had not found any on the list, but within two hours of leaving the storks not one but *two* copies of Paul Fossing's *Glass Vessels Before Glass Blowing* had turned up! I bought them both—one for a single dollar, the other for about 20 dollars. I credit the sweeps with finding the first, the storks with the second.

Holmegaards Glasvaerk, founded in 1825, and Kastrup Glasvaerk, founded in 1847, produce excellent decorative glassware, tableware, and containers of all kinds. Danish craftsmanship excels in the production of top-quality work, whether in glass, porcelain, silver, or anything else!

What chiefly claimed our attention on this last visit to Copenhagen was the delicate work with the torch that I found in several small ateliers where complicated glass apparatus for scientific uses was being made. I can watch for hours the dexterous hands of a master worker who has invented some special technique or tool for performing just one intricate operation. And every hour I learn something new. Hands like these controlled the brushes of Michelangelo and Titian, and carved the masterpieces of Greek sculpture. Equal skill in performance may be common to many workers, but each pair of hands has learned and adopted its own approach and style, and leaves its unique signature on its work. One living picture of a master performer at work is worth more to me than ten thousand words of explanation!

PART II

MY METHODS

Large furnaces tended by groups of highly trained men, such as we saw in Leerdam, obviously do not fit into the life and surroundings of your home and mine. So now, for the first time, I shall describe in detail my own unique methods of blowing, sculpting, and shaping glass—methods I have developed and practiced in my own studio for over 20 years.

What I have done in my studio, you may learn to do in your own home. With small expense, surrounded by the peace of your own private oasis, you may follow my written guidelines, illustrated with sketches and photographs, and learn to create strong, delicately designed and colored objects that could never be made on the heavy factory iron blowpipes.

I have been asked a thousand times to say in writing just what equipment is needed, where to get it, and how to make a start. Here is all you need to know.

CHAPTER 8

Purchasing Your Equipment

Below is a complete list of the things you need. These may be found at any scientific apparatus company that deals in glass laboratory supplies. Take this book along with you, and show the salesman the picture of simple bench tools for glassworkers shown in Fig. 90. Your needs will be readily identified from this picture. Two outlets are:

Braun Division, Van Waters & Rogers, Inc., Los Angeles, Calif. 90054

Bethlehem Apparatus International Co., Inc., Hellertown, Pennsylvania. 18055

Branch concerns of these or similar companies readily can be found in most large cities throughout the United States.

1. *One National No. 3A blowpipe*   Approximate cost, $14.00

This is a versatile burner. It consumes city gas and air under steady pressure, or city gas and oxygen, or propane (or butane) and oxygen. It is unlikely that you will have a convenient supply of constant-flow air pressure. So, if city gas is available, you should use it together with oxygen. If city gas is not available, you

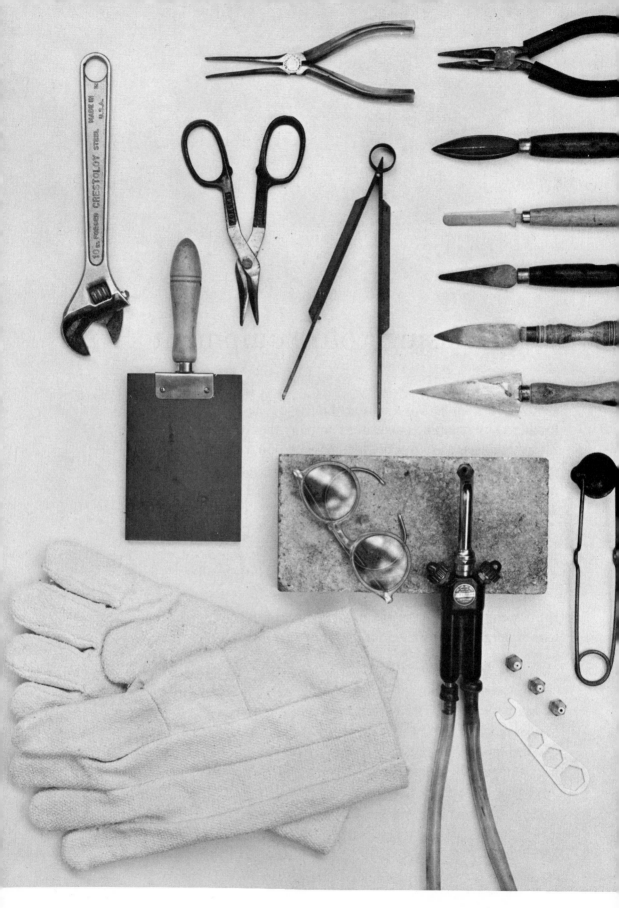

FIGURE 90. Tools for glassblowing.

should use propane (or butane) and oxygen. The propane (or butane) will come in a small 5-gallon tank such as is used on thousands of trailer homes. It must be fitted with a regulator that cuts down the pressure, just as for a trailer tank. The tank should always be placed in the open air under conditions where youngsters cannot possibly meddle with it. Wherever a naked flame is used, such as a gas-burning kitchen stove, you should always have an appropriate kind of fire extinguisher handy. Treat your tanks with the same respect and care that you would give to the tanks on your trailer. Locate them properly, and use them correctly at all times. Fire Department regulations differ from state to state, so be sure that you acquaint yourself with local rules.

Oxygen is supplied in tanks from local dealers. The tank is fitted with a pressure gauge with two dials. One dial indicates how much oxygen is in the tank; the other, the pressure being released through the connecting hose to the burner. This gauge may have to be purchased. If so, the approximate cost should be $25.00.

2. *One carbon flat, with handle*   Approximate cost, $8.00
3. *One pair of glassworker's forceps*   Approximate cost, $8.00
4. *Two brass shaping tools*   Approximate cost, $2.00 ea.
5. *One pair of 10″ shears*   Approximate cost, $2.25
6. *One pair of pliers*   Approximate cost, $2.00
7. *One spark lighter*   Approximate cost, $.35
8. *One pair of "Didymium" goggles*   Approximate cost, $9.00
9. *One small triangular file*   Approximate cost, $.35
10. *Supply of "Pyrex" glass tubing & cane (standard wall tubing)*
    Five lb. of 5 mm.-diameter cane (rod)
    Five lb. of ½″-diameter cane (rod)
    Five lb. of ½″-diameter tubing
11. *Two ordinary firebricks*
12. *Asbestos gloves*
13. *A firm table of metal or wood, about 5 feet × 3 feet, which must be covered with asbestos cloth.*

Your workroom should be airy, but free from drafts, with the ceiling as high as possible. An empty garage or shed often offers suitable conditions. Remember, if you are going to use propane or butane, that *the tank should be out in the open air, where youngsters cannot meddle with it.*

Figure 90 shows a picture of your tools. Always arrange them on your table in orderly fashion and always at the same location, so that you can pick up whatever tool you need without having to think where it is. When you are twirling a blob of molten glass on the end of your blowpipe and are ready to use some tool, there is no time to lose—flowing glass will not wait!

136

CHAPTER 9

Lighting Your Burner

The burner is placed on your table lengthwise, and directly in front of your chair or stool. The tubes connected to the burner trail across the table to the left, and are anchored with a firebrick which holds them securely in place. The brass nozzle of the burner is elevated by the support of a firebrick, so that when lighted the flame is vertical to the table top. Both burner valves are closed. Now, turn on your city gas (or tank gas) at the main outlet. Next turn on the main oxygen tap, and adjust the flow of oxygen to 1 or 2 lb. pressure. Now slowly turn on the burner gas tap, light with your spark lighter, and adjust the yellow flame to about 8 inches in height. Next slowly turn your burner oxygen tap to produce a hot blue flame. Note the yellow cone that rises from the tip of your burner. Adjust the oxygen until this cone is about ¾ inch tall. The blue flame should now be about 6 inches tall. Now turn off the oxygen burner tap, and then the gas tap. Repeat this whole procedure—lighting, adjusting, and turning off—until you handle the burner with complete confidence.

Always light the gas first, before turning on the oxygen.

Always turn off the oxygen before turning off the gas.

Whenever you leave your work table, never leave the burner lighted.

Turn off the gas at its main outlet whenever you leave the room.

Never take any risks, and you will never have any trouble.

When you begin experimenting with glass, please remember that the first thing to learn about any medium that must be manipulated by the skill of hands using simple tools is just how that medium itself behaves and responds as you work with it. For example, there is only one correct way to "plane" soft wood—with the grain. Go counter to the grain and you roughen the wood instead of smoothing it. If copper is being hammered to form a bowl, how much will it curl before the "cold work" imparted by the hammer hardens it to the point where it cannot be shaped further until it has been softened by annealing? Just how malleable is the potter's clay, and just how wet must it be to be drawn out to a fine spout on the wheel?

Every substance has its own unique response to handling just because it is what it is and must follow the laws of its own being. So some good measure of practical familiarity with the unique qualities of glass and its responses to what you do with it must be yours before you can expect to be able to control it to your own ends. Never expect glass to achieve forms or fulfill functions for which it is scientifically and aesthetically unsuited.

As we have learned, there are thousands of varieties of glass with widely differing compositions and properties. The one glass we shall be concerned with is a borosilicate. Its chemistry need not concern us at the moment. The way it behaves as you work with it is all that matters for the time being. It is a variety of "Pyrex" (a patented name) made by Corning.

Pyrex begins to soften at about 840 degrees Centigrade. Glass has no definite melting point. This softening point is considerably higher than that of window glass or most tableware. Pyrex has a low coefficient of expansion, which is to say that it expands comparatively little when heated, and, conversely, it contracts very little when cooled. These and other properties make Pyrex the very best

138

glass for our present purposes. Do not attempt to mix Pyrex with any other glasses. Although they may appear to mix when in the molten state, they will always pull apart when cooled to room temperature. They are what we call "incompatible"—like many people!

All glasses must be cooled slowly from high temperatures to prevent strains from developing which result in cracking. Pyrex is no exception to this rule.

Finally, please remember this: anyone who watches an experienced lampworker dexterously manipulating his tubes and rods in and around the torch may well conclude that it is something almost anyone can do right away. It *is* something that almost anyone can learn to do, but not right away.

CHAPTER 10

Experiments with Torch and Glass Blowpipe

EXPERIMENT ONE (Fig. 91)

Introduce the jagged tip of a 12-inch-long rod 5 mm. in diameter into the flame of your torch above the yellow cone, and rotate the rod evenly between thumbs and fingers of both hands. Notice that the sharp edge of the glass begins to melt. Continue heating until the whole end of the rod is fused for a distance of about ¼ inch. Allow it to cool. Observe that the end of the rod is now quite smooth and round. It has been re-shaped and "fire-polished."

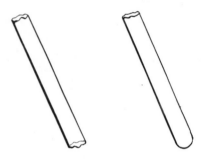

FIGURE 91. Rods.

EXPERIMENT TWO (Fig. 92)

Proceed as in Experiment One, but this time use a glass tube. Note that the heat seals the end of the tube round and smooth. You have now learned by experience a basic fact about the melting of the ends of glass tubes and rods while rotating

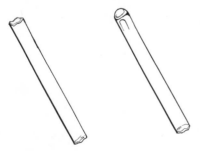

FIGURE 92. Tubes.

them evenly: the new shape that the heat has given the tip is always round and smooth!

Important Note: By "rotating" we mean turning the rod or tube around and around, smoothly and evenly. It is most important to acquire steadiness of hand movement as you manipulate molten glass in the flame. In large measure, this will determine your degree of skill and success in all later phases of more complicated techniques of blowing and shaping. So find a natural, comfortable way of handling your tubes and rods, using both hands.

EXPERIMENT THREE (Fig. 93)

Introduce the last inch of a ½-inch glass rod into the flame above the yellow cone and hold it perfectly still, without rotating. As the glass melts, it will be pulled by the force of gravity toward the earth. Soon a pear-shaped drop will be dangling on a thread of glass.

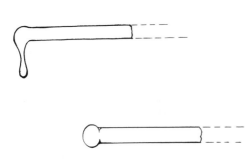

FIGURE 93. Rods.

Repeat the experiment, but this time rotate the inch of glass evenly in the flame, while inclining the rod slightly so that the heated tip is higher than the cool end nearest your body. Notice that the molten glass flows toward you, thickening the rod and taking the form of a sphere. Your rotary motion has allowed gravity to exert its pull evenly, while compelling the molten glass to flow toward you and form a sphere.

Repeat this experiment, using this time a piece of ½-inch tubing. The glass will melt, sealing the end of the tube, and the wall of the tube nearest the sealed end will thicken. If heating is prolonged, you will get a blob of solid glass on the end of your tube.

141

EXPERIMENT FOUR (Fig. 94)

Now take a 15-inch length of ½-inch tubing, smooth the tip of one end in the flame, and allow it to cool. You have now made a glass blowpipe such as you will be using in all your later work. The smoothed, fire-polished end will be your mouthpiece for blowing. Always be sure that this mouthpiece is quite cold before you put it in your mouth.

Now introduce the first half-inch of the unsmoothed end into the

FIGURE 94. Tube.

flame and rotate it evenly. The glass will melt, sealing the end of the tube, and the walls nearest the end will thicken. Remove from the flame and blow quickly through the mouthpiece. The soft glass will expand into a paper-thin bubble which probably will burst. Expanding molten glass by controlled pressure of the breath is the basic procedure in making blown hollow ware.

Naturally, the glass may be made too hot and ductile for controlled blowing. In that event, the resulting bubble will be large, irregular, paper thin, and almost always will burst. If, on the other hand, the glass is too cold and rigid, you will not be able to make it expand no matter how hard you blow. You will quickly come to know by experience the right temperature for controlled blowing and the right pressure to exert with your breath.

142

EXPERIMENT FIVE (Figs. 95, 96)

Once again heat-seal the end of your blowpipe and clamp your right thumb over the hole in the mouthpiece while rotating evenly (as shown in Fig. 95). The air trapped inside the blowpipe will

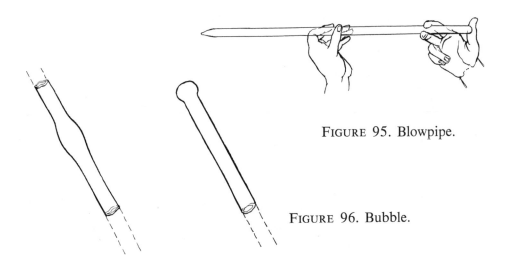

FIGURE 95. Blowpipe.

FIGURE 96. Bubble.

expand and will cause the molten glass to expand also. A small bubble will be blown by the hot trapped air without using any mouth-blowing (Fig. 96).

EXPERIMENT SIX (Fig. 97)

Repeat Experiment Five, but this time heat a full inch of the end of the blowpipe. Remove from the flame, still rotating evenly, and blow gently to form a bubble about 1¼ inches in diameter (Fig. 97). The wall of the bubble will be thin and fragile, but if you have performed the experiment correctly, the bubble will be an almost perfect sphere. Practice this procedure until you have mastered it. By inclining your blowpipe (as in Experiment 3), and so incorporating more glass into the thickened wall, you will be able

143

to make the wall of the bubble stronger, and the bubble bigger. You should stay with this part of your experimentation, performing the same thing many times. Train your eye to notice precisely

Figure 97. Blowpipe.

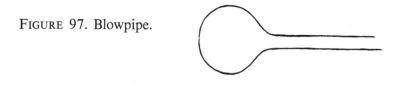

what the flame is doing to the glass, and train your hands until they automatically behave in the right way to control the flow of glass.

EXPERIMENT SEVEN (Fig. 98)

Figure 98 shows a strong bubble to which "hobnails" of glass have been fused. Follow this procedure: blow a strong-walled bubble about 1½ inches in diameter. Now, holding the blowpipe in the left hand and taking care to keep the wall of the bubble near to but just outside the flame, touch the molten tip of a 5-mm. rod, which you hold in your right hand, to the wall of the bubble and pull the rod away. A small blob of solid glass from the rod will be left adhering to the bubble wall. Proceed to encircle the bubble with a series of blobs, as shown in Fig. 98. These blobs must be spaced evenly and similar in size. When the pattern (Fig. 98) is completed, the bubble is next rotated evenly in the flame to melt the hobnails securely to its wall. This fusion may decrease the size of the bubble, and it may have to be expanded by gentle blowing. Next, turn off the oxygen at the burner tap and rotate the bubble

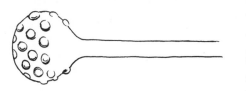

Figure 98. Hobnails.

144

in the yellow carbon flame until the piece is covered with black carbon. This allows the bubble to cool slowly and prevents possible cracks. Now cool to room temperature by resting the blackened bubble on your carbon marver. Wipe off the black carbon with soft cloth, and you will discover a beautiful small object in glass.

EXPERIMENT EIGHT

Proceed as in Experiment Seven until you have covered the bubble with hobnails. Now rotate the bubble in the flame until all the hobnails are completely fused into the wall. During this procedure you must keep trapping and releasing the air inside the blowpipe by closing the hole in the mouthpiece with your right thumb (as shown in Fig. 95), and then taking it off. This alternating air pressure inside the blowpipe will prevent the bubble from collapsing. A final gentle blowing will restore the bubble to its original size, but now with a smooth wall. Once more cool in the carbon flame and on the marver. When you wipe away the black carbon you will find a beautiful pattern sunk in the wall (as shown in Fig. 99a).

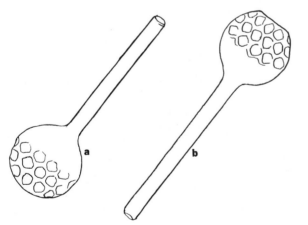

FIGURE 99. Tube with hobnails.

145

EXPERIMENT NINE (Fig. 99b)

Take the bubble you last made, and soften a small area of the extreme end while rotating it evenly and steadily in the flame. Now press the softened part on your marver while holding the blowpipe vertical to the surface of the marver. The flattened surface will become the standing base of a small bottle (see Fig. 99b). Cool off in the carbon flame and on the marver. To finish your first bottle, nick the blowpipe 2 or 3 inches above the bubble with your three-cornered file, then hold the blowpipe in a cloth and crack off by exerting sudden pressure as if you would bend the tube. Smooth rough end in the flame, and flare out with the flaring tool (Fig. 100). This first bottle should resemble Fig. 99b.

FIGURE 100. Flaring tool.

EXPERIMENT TEN (Figs. 101a, b, c)

Using both hands, hold a 15-inch tube at the ends between the fingers and the thumbs. While rotating evenly in a horizontal position, introduce an area about 5 inches from one end into the flame. As the tube begins to soften, press gently and evenly from both ends to thicken the wall of the tube (Fig. 101a). Remove from the flame

FIGURE 101. Tubes.

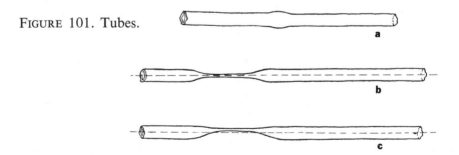

a

b

c

146

and draw the two ends apart along their original common axis, to form a narrow section about ⅛ inch in diameter (Fig. 101b). The narrowed section should be coaxial with the original tube. Uneven heating or pulling will produce the wrong shape (shown in Fig. 101c). Now fuse off all but 2 inches of the original tube from the

FIGURE 102. Tubes.

FIGURE 103. Bubble.

shorter end, and then make a mouthpiece at the opposite end, so that your piece will resemble Fig. 102. Now heat all the wide-diameter tube on the working end, and blow a bubble as shown in Fig. 103. This bubble may be left plain, or it may be ornamented with hobnail or other pattern. Then the narrowed tube nearest the long part of the blowpipe is fused off in the flame. To this fused end add a hook made of 5-mm. rod, as shown in Fig. 104. You have now made a simple, but very effective, Christmas tree hanging ornament. If you turn your imagination loose, you can make such ornaments in great variety for your next Christmas festivities.

FIGURE 104. Christmas tree ornament.

147

FIGURE 105. Christmas tree ornament.

FIGURE 106.

FIGURE 107.

FIGURE 108.

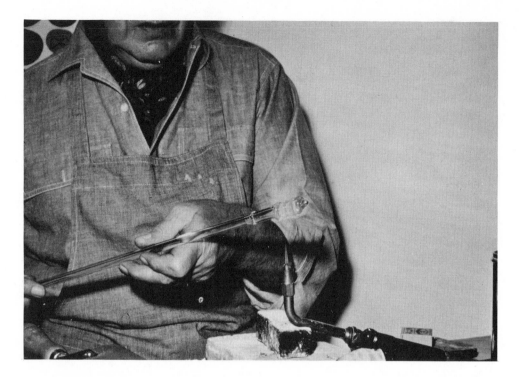

FIGURE 109.

FIGURE 110.

FIGURE 111.

Figure 112.

Figure 113.

FIGURE 114.

FIGURE 115.

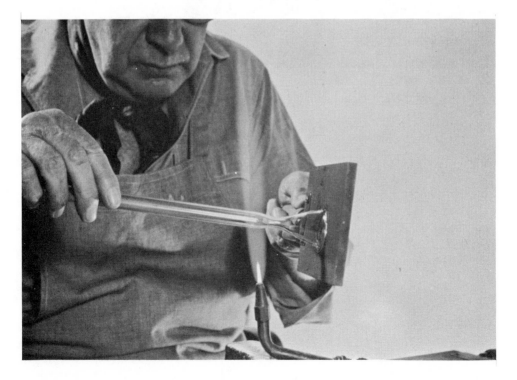

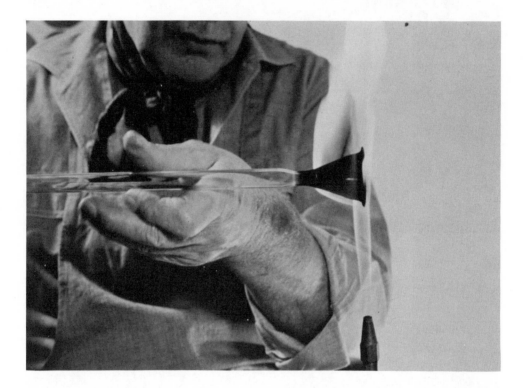

FIGURE 116.

Figure 117.

Figure 118.

FIGURE 119.

FIGURE 120.

FIGURE 121.

FIGURE 122.

FIGURE 123.

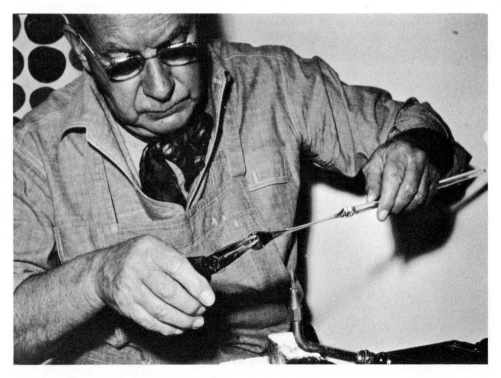

FIGURE 124.

The first 10 experiments are designed to familiarize you with the behavior of glass and its manipulation in its simplest forms. By now you will have made many important discoveries while translating my written guidance into your own individual performance. Achieving skill in action is a highly individual matter. No two people adopt exactly the same approach or style in doing anything. You are finding out how to work in your own way, comfortably and naturally adjusting your bodily position and the actions of hands and breath to cooperate with the laws that govern flowing glass. By so doing you are learning to control a flowing material, to fulfill your own designs and purposes. By repeating the foregoing experiments you are laying the groundwork for all your later successes.

Now you must take a further step that will make larger pieces possible. Please study Fig. 125 carefully. It shows 8 models, numbered from left to right. Number 1 shows the working end of a blowpipe. Number 2 is that same blowpipe end, covered with coils of 5-mm. rod. This is done as follows:

Hold the blowpipe in the left hand with the mouthpiece pointed under your left armpit, and heat the last 2 inches in the flame until molten glass adheres to the wall. Now, while rotating close to but just outside the flame, adhere the tip of a 5-mm. rod at a point 2 inches from the end, and begin to trail molten glass from the rod around the slowly rotating tube (counterclockwise). Each coil should fit snugly against the last, forming a spiral that completely covers the 2 inches of the working end. Note that thin threads of air are trapped between the coils. These threads will take the form of small air bubbles that remain incorporated in the wall after fusing to stage three (see Fig. 125). This trapping of air may or may not be desired. I like to introduce air bubbles into many of my pieces for added interest and broken light-transmission in the finished piece. They add beauty and a touch of the romantic to the hand-wrought imperfections of the piece.

Number 3 shows the piece after the coils are completely fused

160

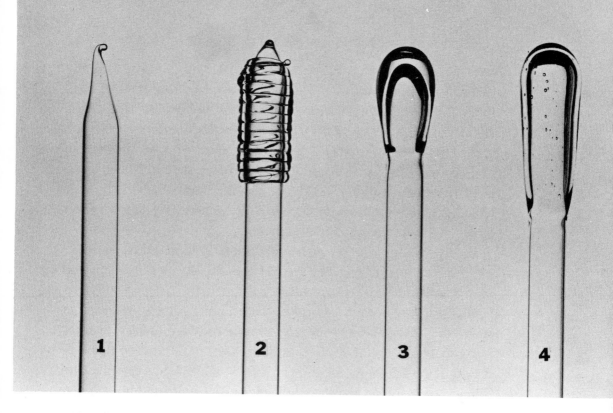

FIGURE 125. Author's series.

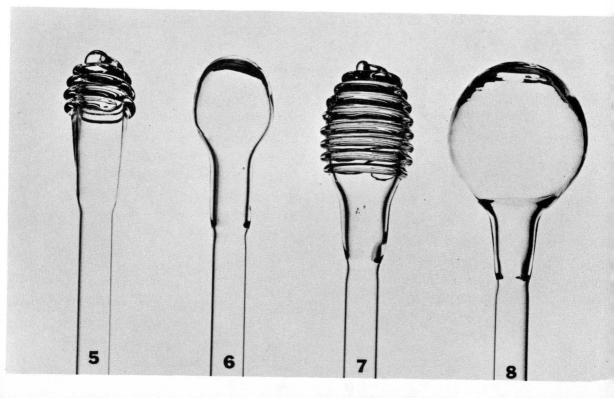

into the wall. Number 4 is achieved by holding Number 3 almost vertically in the flame, and allowing the glass to elongate while maintaining an even interior shape of the air pocket. Number 5 shows further coils added to Number 4. This time the coils are spaced so that they do not touch one another. (No further air bubbles will have been added.) In Number 6 the coils have again been fused in. Number 7 shows that still more coils have been added, and in Number 8 these coils have been fused and the bubble blown to a diameter of about 3½ inches.

By these additions of evenly distributed, solid glass, we have built up the thickness of the wall of the bubble, step by step, and have a bubble with a strong wall.

If a still larger piece of hollow ware is to be made, we start at stage Number 4, and add successively one or two more sets of coils, fusing between each addition. In doing this, care must be taken to maintain the size of the interior air cavity. This means that the wall is now very thick. When the whole piece is at uniform high temperature throughout, remove from the flame, hang in a perpendicular position, and blow to form a bubble 4 to 5 inches in diameter. Cool in the carbon flame and on the marver. This bubble may be left spherical in shape, or the end two-thirds may be softened and marvered. The base may then be flattened on the marver as before. We now have a most useful vase for flowers.

Next let us find out just how colored glass is made.

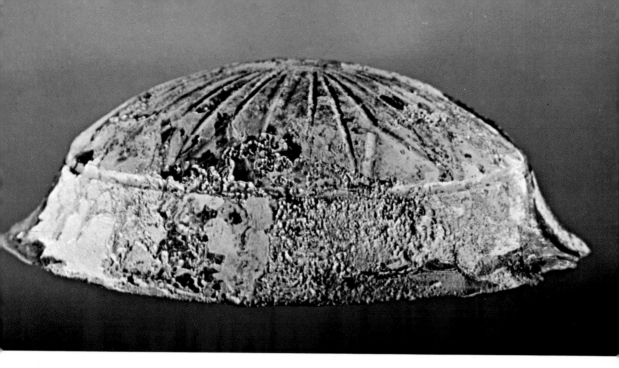

1. Bowl. Near East. Possibly late first millennium B.C. or pre-Islamic. *Courtesy, The Corning Museum of Glass, Corning, N. Y.*

2. Chalice. Roman Empire (c. 1st century A.D.). *Courtesy, The Corning Museum of Glass, Corning, N. Y.*

3. Roman glass group. *Left to right:* Daphne Vase, enameled and gilded, portraying the story of Daphne and Apollo; cameo glass cup, carved with a frieze depicting the worship of the god, Priapus; "Millefiori" (meaning a thousand flowers) bowl. All made in Italy and the Near East (c. 1st–3rd century A.D.). *Courtesy, The Corning Museum of Glass, Corning, N.Y.*

4. Ewer of pale blue facet-cut glass. Parthian or possibly early Sassanian (3rd or 4th century A.D.). *Courtesy, The Corning Museum of Glass, Corning, N.Y.*

5. Enameled armorial beaker. Germany, probably Saxony (1671). *Courtesy, The Corning Museum of Glass, Corning, N. Y.*

6. Vase. England, possibly Bristol (c. 1770–1780). *Courtesy, The Corning Museum of Glass, Corning, N. Y.*

7. Sugar bowl. New Jersey, attributed to Wistarberg or Glassboro (c. 1740–1780). *Courtesy, The Corning Museum of Glass, Corning, N. Y.*

8. Enameled goblet. Venice (first quarter, 16th century). *Courtesy, The Corning Museum of Glass, Corning, N. Y.*

9. My models made while teaching.

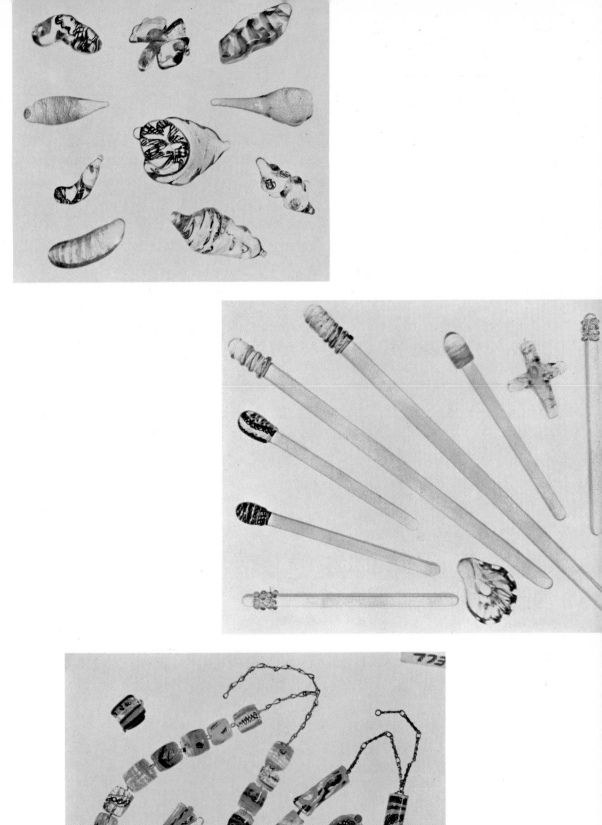

CHAPTER **11**

Making Colored
Snake Thread

Colors in glass result from small additions of various metallic oxides. Cobalt oxide produces blue. Tin oxide produces milk-white.
Chromium oxide produces green. Copper oxide produces red. A
convenient rough-and-ready but highly satisfactory bench method
of adding one or another of these oxides to glass is the following:

Seal one end of a 3-inch length of ½-inch tubing in the flame,
and place inside it a few grains of cobalt oxide, which is black.
Fuse the closed end of this tube to the end of a 15-inch-long, solid
rod, ½ inch in diameter (see Fig. 126). Now melt the tube containing the oxide, allowing the glass to flow over and cover the
oxide. Heat the whole mass to form an irregular lump. Now attach
another 15-inch rod to the lump and begin to rotate the two rods in
opposite directions, so as to mix the oxide thoroughly with the glass
(see Fig. 127). Continue this mixing in the hottest flame until a
smooth blue color has been imparted evenly to the whole lump.
When the outside contour of the colored glass is smooth and globular, remove from the flame and pull the rods apart, so that a thin
rod about ⅛ inch in diameter is stretched between them. The den-
sity of the blue color will depend on the amount of the cobalt

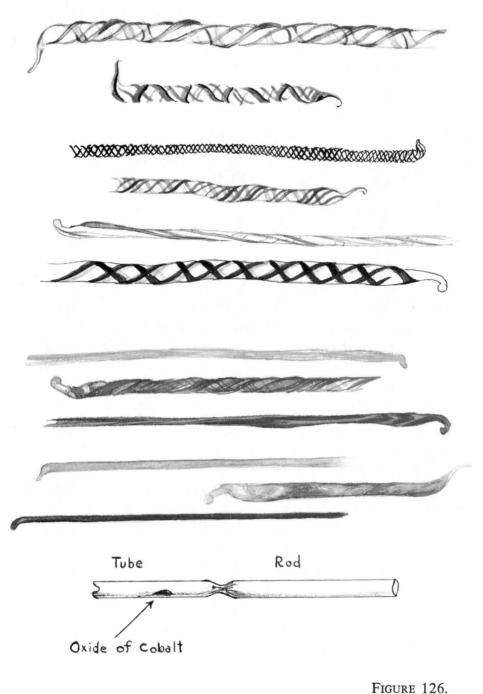

Tube   Rod

Oxide of Cobalt

FIGURE 126.

oxide used and the amount of the water-white glass with which it has been mixed. This fine rod should be cut into 12-inch lengths in flame for later use.

This thin, hand-spun, pigmented rod we call "snake thread" in honor of the ancient Egyptians, who first learned how to make it. They used this kind of snake thread to make colored designs on their amphora and other containers. You may use it in the same manner, for snake thread constitutes a kind of paintbrush that adds color to your creation through the heat of the flame in any design that you wish to make. By mixing a little tin oxide with the cobalt oxide, you can make any shade of pastel blue. The other oxides may be mixed with glass in the same manner, adding a nice range of colors to use on your pieces. I suggest that you make quite a collection of snake thread in varying diameters and colors.

MAKING SNAKE THREAD CONTAINING A COLOR TWIST (Figs. 128a and b)

Take a 15-inch length of ½-inch rod, heat the first 2 inches of one end, and point slightly on the marver by rolling. Now trail six parallel lines of deep blue snake thread, from the point along the axis of the rod (Fig. 128a). These must be spaced evenly around the rod over the heated area. Heat and marver until the snake thread has been completely incorporated into the surface of the rod.

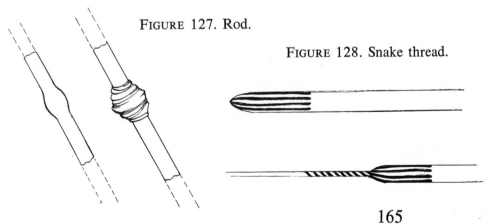

FIGURE 127. Rod.

FIGURE 128. Snake thread.

165

Now attach a length of 5-mm. rod to the point. Rotating the rod evenly with the left hand, apply heat to the point where the thick rod begins to narrow, while rotating the 5-mm. rod with the right hand and exerting a slight, but constant, pull away from the point being heated. Note that the blue snake thread is being twisted around the new thread that you are spinning from the thick rod. Proceed until all the color on the thick rod has been used up. You may now cut the thin twist snake thread into lengths of about 12 inches as before. The pattern of the twist may be varied by changing the number of blue threads on the big rod, by the diameter of the color thread, and by the speed of rotation and the pull on the thin rod. Naturally, the twist snake thread may be made of two or more colors and the uses to which it may be put are endless. (See Fig. 126.)

I have picked at random and sketched a few items from my collection of small pieces made through the years. They are reproduced here not necessarily to be imitated, but merely to hint at the great variety of objects that can be fashioned from glass.

Now that you are becoming more skillful, be more audacious as well! Experiment freely with your own ideas. You will learn from your mistakes no less than from your successes. Never stop trying. I once asked a highly skilled professional—a master glassworker in a famous factory—if he could take a blueprint and translate the design into actuality at the first attempt. He told me, "No, I usually make sixteen or seventeen tries, and throw the pieces back into the furnace. But after that I can turn them out, one after another, so much alike that only with calipers can you tell the difference."

The sculptured tray (Fig. 129) is made of different shades of blue, and was shaped by means of heavy pliers and chisels while red-hot. The abstract form (Fig. 130) suggested itself while I was wandering about the Arizona desert looking at strange cactus forms. It was made from very thick glass rod, and shaped by cutting and twisting the molten glass in a fashion impossible to describe

166

in words. But it isn't impossible for you to do if you use the skill you have gained plus a good measure of ingenuity.

Figure 131 is a far cry from the richly embroidered church vestments I was admiring one day in Notre Dame Cathedral in Paris. Just the same, it was there that I got the idea of making a glass

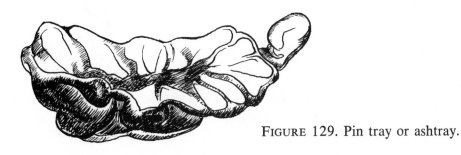

FIGURE 129. Pin tray or ashtray.

sketch of some vestments standing up on their own, minus a wearer. I added a mitre. For 10 years this little piece has attracted much comment from visitors to my studio. The design is in blue twist. The knobs shown in Fig. 132 are of solid water-white glass with colored designs in blue and sepia twist. The doorknobs inside my

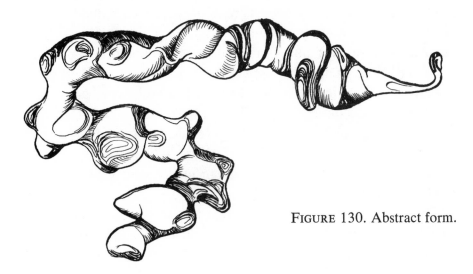

FIGURE 130. Abstract form.

167

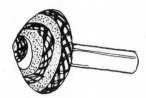

FIGURE 132.
Glass doorknobs.

FIGURE 131. Vestments in glass.

studio are fashioned in this way. They are most effective. Figure 133 shows a strong thick bubble with green-and-white twist designs. I use such pieces for lamp finials, since they play with light so beautifully. I also seal them close to the bubble and my wife floats them among flowers and leaves in a large glass table bowl along with smaller and larger bubbles.

I never saw a live creature exactly like this snail shown in Fig. 134. (Who knows?—you may find one like it in the garden some day.) Colored twist is coiled to make the shell. The slithering body, neck, and horns are clear glass. Question: Do snails have necks? Frankly, I don't know.

In the color insert is shown a group of stirrers and muddlers for drinks. These are simply ½-inch rods, fire-polished at one end (cooled very slowly) and ornamented with color designs at the other end. Your friends will appreciate them as gifts at all seasons.

Also illustrated in the color insert are two strings of heavy, colored, primitive-looking beads. These are made by coiling snake thread or twist, appropriate to the desired design, on the end of the blowpipe, fusing and separating. If beads hold a special interest for you, as they do for many, you can make innumerable shapes by starting with this basic technique.

The solid objects illustrated in the color insert are examples of smooth "touch pieces." They are made to handle for pure tactile pleasure. Men and women in all civilizations have used touch

168

FIGURE 133. Bubble.

FIGURE 134. Snail.

pieces of one sort or another to soothe the nerves and so induce relaxed composure—something for worried executives and exasperated housewives. In ancient Greece, touch pieces strung on strings (which the Greeks call Koumpologia) and made of polished hardwood, mother-of-pearl, or amber, sometimes strangely shaped, were in common use. I found them in modern Athens, fulfilling their ancient purpose as harmless tranquilizers.

Now let me describe in detail some of these techniques which you are ready to try.

CHAPTER 12

Beads

Trail colored snake thread around a ½-inch diameter blowpipe, leaving ¼ inch of clear glass at the very tip (Figs. 135 and 136).

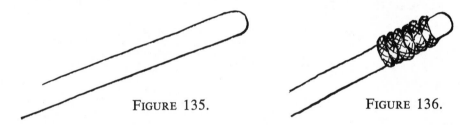

FIGURE 135.   FIGURE 136.

Apply the torch flame to the colored area, while rotating evenly, until the dividing lines between the circles of the snake thread disappear, and the whole surface is smooth and fire-polished (Figs. 137 and 138). Your choice of colors, and the order in which you have trailed them around the blowpipe, have set the final appearance of your finished bead. The outside diameter of the bead should now be about the same as the diameter of the blowpipe—½ inch.

Now heat the extreme tip of the clear glass (Fig. 138), and blow out into a paper-thin bubble (Fig. 139). Discard the paper-

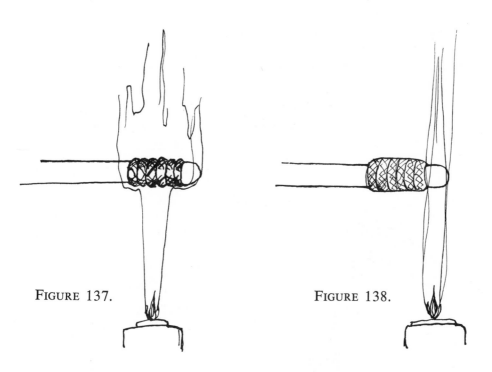

FIGURE 137.

FIGURE 138.

thin glass, and rotate the jagged edge of the bead in the flame (Fig. 140). Trim away the softened glass with shears (Fig. 141), and fire-polish (Fig. 142), checking for correct diameter of the

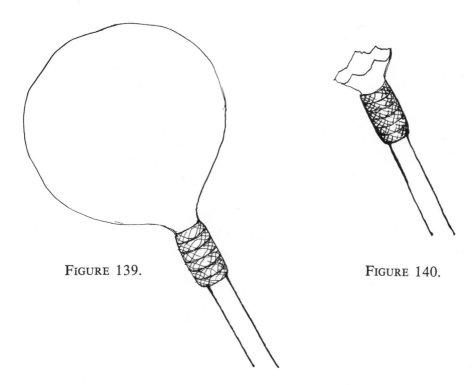

FIGURE 139.

FIGURE 140.

hole through the bead with the carbon stick. If too large, the hole may be reduced by marvering (Fig. 143).

Check the hole once more with the carbon stick (Fig. 144). Now attach a 5-mm. rod in the manner shown in Fig. 145. Holding

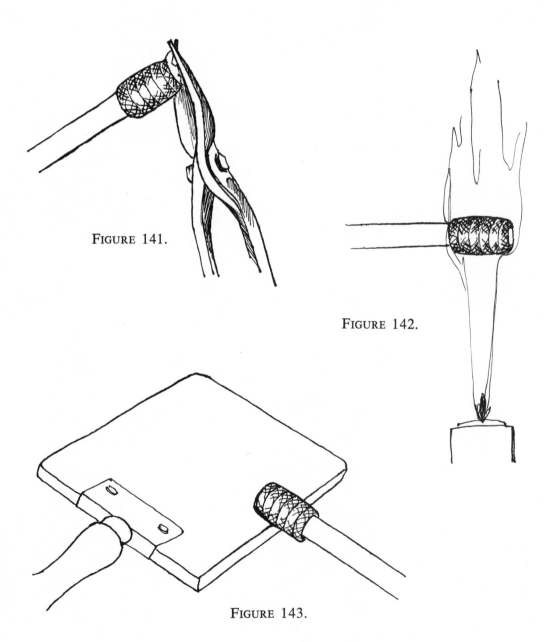

FIGURE 141.

FIGURE 142.

FIGURE 143.

the 5-mm. rod, remove the bead from the blowpipe in the flame (Fig. 146). Crack the pointed end with tweezers (Fig. 147), open up the hole with the brass shaper (Fig. 148), taking care not to put the shaper into the flame, and again trim with the shears.

FIGURE 144.

FIGURE 145.

FIGURE 146.

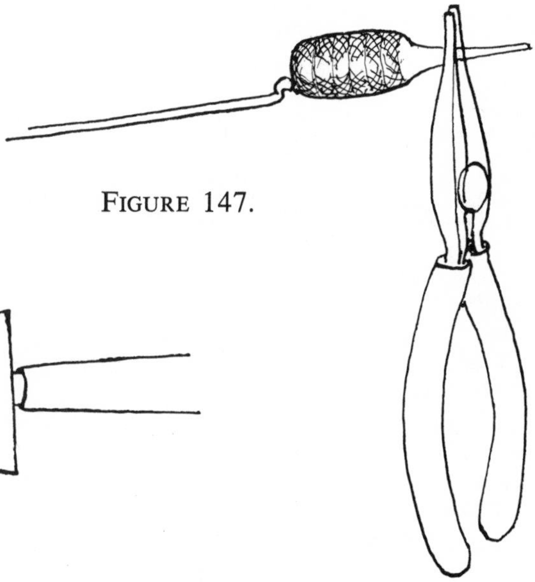

FIGURE 147.

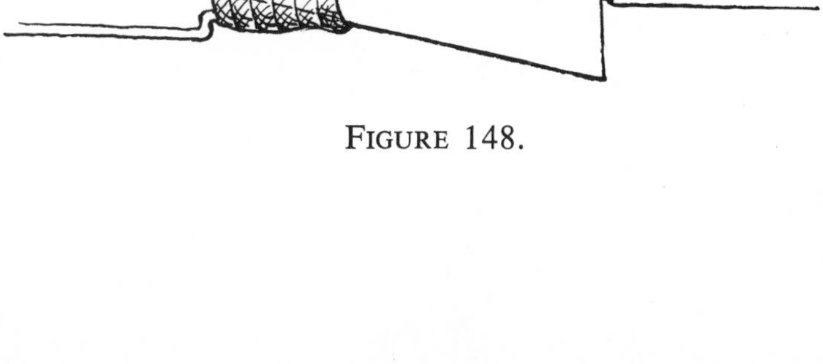

FIGURE 148.

Once more check the inside diameter of the hole with the carbon stick. Now bring the entire bead to a dull red heat (Fig. 149), and adjust any irregularities on the marver (Figs. 150 and 151). Check the hole with the carbon stick (Figs. 152 and 153). Now make as many beads as you want.

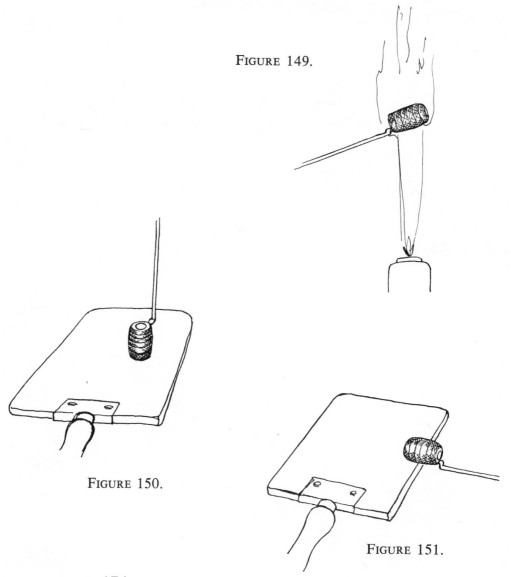

FIGURE 149.

FIGURE 150.

FIGURE 151.

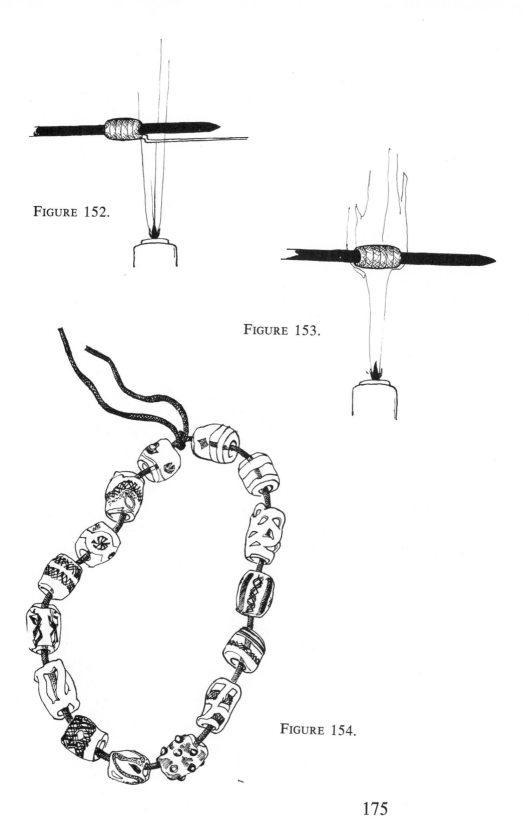

FIGURE 152.

FIGURE 153.

FIGURE 154.

175

CHAPTER 13

Cravettes

These are used as scarf holders. The opposite points of a square silk (or other) scarf can be drawn through the cravette, either from one side or from opposite sides, and adjusted to hold the scarf together neatly. The cravette will not slip off the scarf if adjusted properly.

Heat 2 to 3 inches of the end of a 5-mm. rod, and trail colored snake threads in successive layers to form a flat band about 2½ inches long and 1 inch wide (Figs. 155–157). Now heat the end half of this band, fusing all the layers of snake thread together, and squeeze with flat-nosed pliers to form perfectly flat surfaces (Fig. 158).

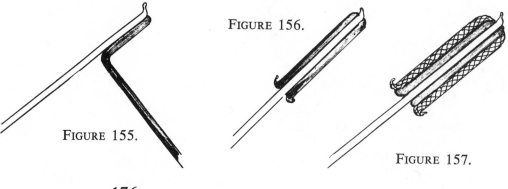

FIGURE 156.

FIGURE 155.

FIGURE 157.

Cravettes

Now attach a 5-mm. rod to this finished end, remove the rod from the other end (Fig. 160), and proceed to heat and squeeze the second half of the band to match the first (Fig. 161). Now,

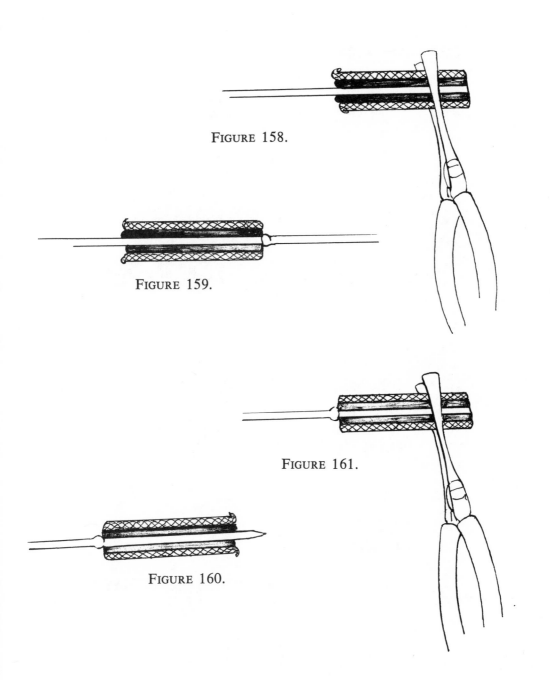

FIGURE 158.

FIGURE 159.

FIGURE 161.

FIGURE 160.

with rods attached to both ends (Fig. 162), return the whole flat band to the flame—heating evenly throughout, and slowly shaping the flat band into a horseshoe as you manipulate the two holding rods (Fig. 163).

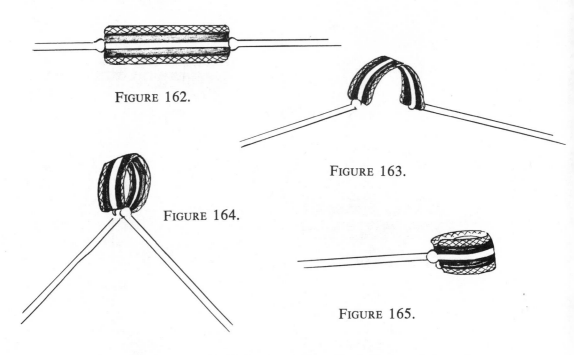

Figure 162.

Figure 163.

Figure 164.

Figure 165.

Close the open end of the horseshoe by fusing together the extreme tips of the two holding rods (Fig. 164). Now remove one of the rods, and fuse it to a point on the edge of the horseshoe band (Figs. 165 and 166). Place the carbon stick through the nearly finished cravette.

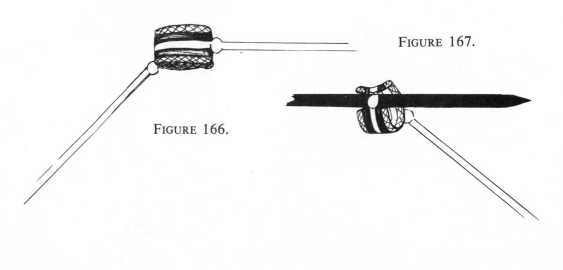

Figure 167.

Figure 166.

Cravettes

Figure 167 illustrates the clear glass drop that links the two ends of the horseshoe.

Now remove the remaining rod in fine flame, leaving a clear drop of glass as shown in Fig. 168. While it is on the carbon stick, heat

FIGURE 168.

the entire cravette evenly to a dull red, and shape to its final form if the shape has become distorted. Anneal in the yellow flame (without oxygen) until the entire piece is thickly coated with carbon. Place in the cooling tin until the piece is at room temperature.

Cravettes of many sizes, shapes, and color designs can be made by this method. Two sketches of pieces I have made are shown in Figs. 169 and 170.

FIGURE 170.

FIGURE 169.

179

CHAPTER 14

Goblets

To make the simplest form of goblet, and so become familiar with the general basic technique, proceed as shown in Fig. 125 as far as Number 6. Since one picture is worth ten thousand words (old Chinese proverb), I think that you will find the nine illustrations of myself making a simple goblet of great practical help (see Figs. 171–179).

Now heat the narrow end closest to the blowpipe to a lively red, and, holding the blowpipe lightly with finger and thumb of the right hand, allow gravity to pull it into the perpendicular position and draw the softened glass downward, thus narrowing what will become the stem of the goblet to the desired diameter. The wall of the stem, after the desired outside diameter has been achieved, should be not less than $\frac{1}{16}$ inch thick. This will give sufficient strength to the stem, and ensure a usable goblet.

Now add more coils of glass to the area that will become the bowl of the goblet (as shown in Fig. 125, Number 7). Repeat, adding glass as many times as required to blow to the desired size, shape, and strength (Fig. 181).

Next, heat the extreme end of the bubble (bowl) to a lively

180

FIGURE 171.

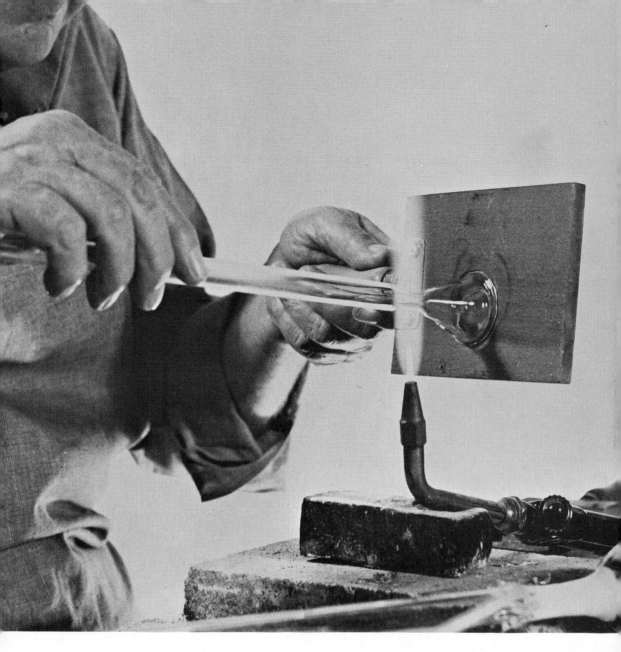

FIGURE 173.

FIGURE 172.

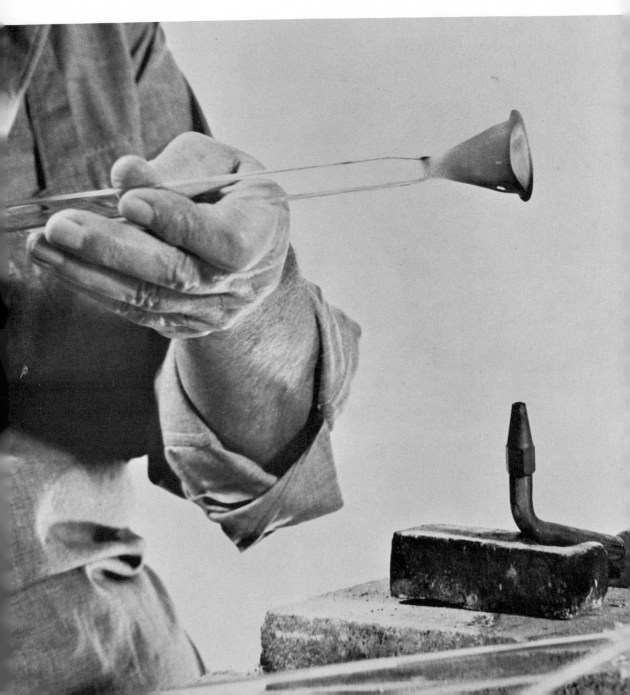

FIGURE 174.

FIGURE 175.

FIGURE 177.

FIGURE 176.

FIGURE 178.

FIGURE 179.

FIGURE 180. (*Photo by Nora R. Klynjan.*)

red, and blow out the end (Fig. 182). Remove the paper-thin blown-out portion, and heat the jagged edge of the lip, while rotating, then trim with shears (Fig. 183). Fire-polish the trimmed

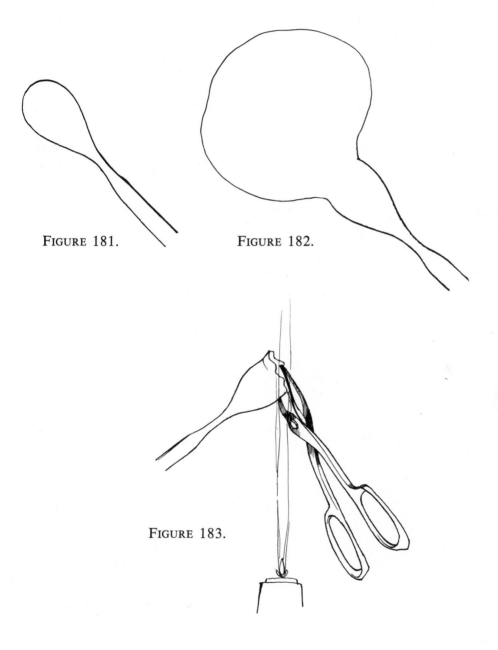

FIGURE 181.

FIGURE 182.

FIGURE 183.

lip (Fig. 184), then blacken in carbon flame and allow to cool. Remove the black carbon with a cloth. Now remove the half-finished goblet from the blowpipe in the flame, and seal the lower end of stem (Fig. 185).

Heat the tip of a 15-inch-long, 5-mm. rod to the same intensity of red heat as the tip of the sealed stem, and bring the two together

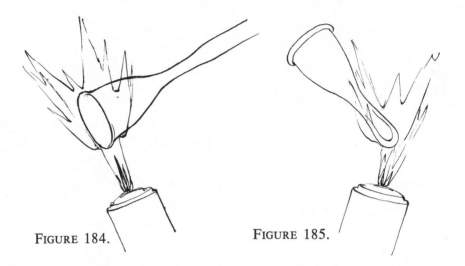

FIGURE 184.   FIGURE 185.

in the flame. The goblet is held in the left hand around its lip. Now start to coil the red-hot rod around and around the stem to form a foot for the goblet (Fig. 186). (The rod is held in the right hand—

FIGURE 186.

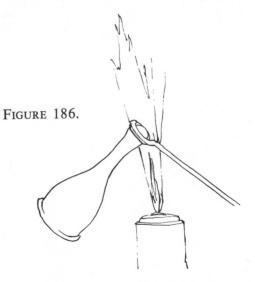

192

the left hand is still holding the goblet by the lip.) The coiling process consists in feeding the rod through the flame with the right hand, while winding the red-hot softened glass onto the foot. This is done by rotating the goblet counterclockwise at the speed necessary to distribute the soft glass in coils of regular thickness. Widen the diameter of the foot to correspond with the diameter of the lip (Fig. 187).

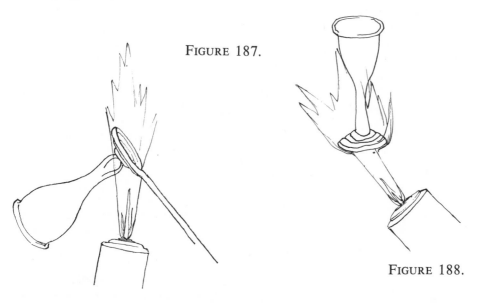

Figure 187.

Figure 188.

When the desired diameter of the foot has been achieved, separate the remainder of the straight rod from the foot in the flame. Now hold the goblet by the lip in the right hand, and proceed to rotate, keeping the under side of the foot in the flame. Continue rotating, as in Figs. 188 and 189, until all the coils are thoroughly fused together. In doing this, it is not necessary to obliterate completely the spiral pattern of the coils. Such a pattern causes a delightful play of light in the finished piece.

The foot will now be red-hot throughout, and in a pliable condition. This is the moment to make certain that it will cool and harden at right angles to the axis of the stem by pressing it gently on the surface of the marver, while the marver is held at eye level (Figs. 190 and 191). This step takes some practice. You may have to heat the foot more than once to a pliable condition before you succeed in achieving perpendicularity of the stem. The moment you see that the goblet stands up straight on the marver, return

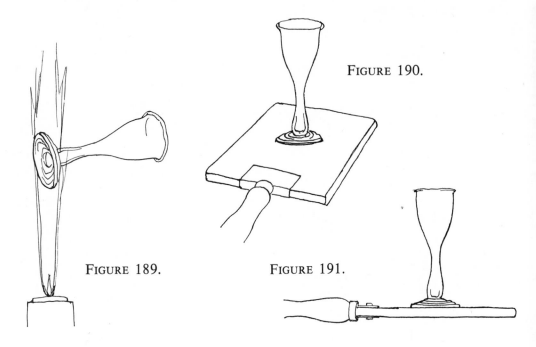

FIGURE 190.

FIGURE 189.   FIGURE 191.

the foot to the flame and rotate, while gradually reducing the oxygen to the torch, and finally turning the oxygen off. Continue rotating the foot in the yellow carbon flame until it is covered with a heavy layer of carbon (Fig. 192). Now place the goblet in an asbestos-lined tin can, and cool to room temperature (Fig. 193).

After the goblet has cooled to room temperature, remove the carbon soot with a cloth and wash in luke-warm, soapy water. Rinse thoroughly. After that proceed to drink a toast to your new achievement out of your very first goblet. You might even raise a second glass to me!

194

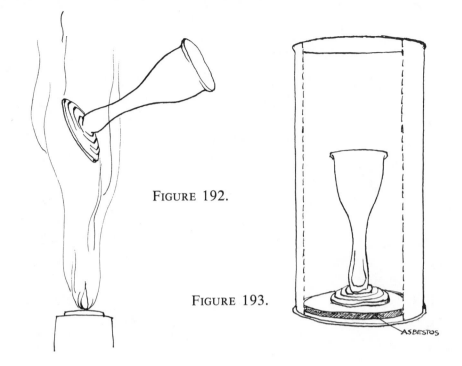

FIGURE 192.

FIGURE 193.

ASBESTOS

Now that you have fashioned your first simple goblet, have put it to appropriate use, and have pointed out to your family and friends that it is all in one piece, without cracks, and stands upright on its sturdy foot, I suggest that you make several more of the same simple variety in order to master thoroughly the necessary steps in its creation. Each achievement will be easier than the last, and soon you will be ready to try your hand at more ambitious creations of widely differing shapes with additions of color.

GOBLETS WITH COLOR DESIGNS

Before you embark on this new adventure, I suggest that you study carefully the color pictures and also the sketches of pieces I have selected from my own collection (Figs. 194–205). It might be good thinking on your part to choose the simplest of these—that is, one closest to the shapes you have already made, but now with the addition of color thread fused into the surface of the bowl, then try to make one substantially like it. Perhaps you will decide, very wisely, on the one shown in Fig. 197. To make this, a simple spiral of thin blue snake thread is coiled around the bowl at stage 6 in Fig. 125. This thread is completely fused into the wall of the bubble before adding the final water-white coils to achieve the result shown in Fig. 181. Then proceed to finish the goblet by the steps you took to make your first one. The blue coil will be set permanently in the bowl of the goblet.

In your next goblet, blue can be added by touching the red-hot tip of a snake thread to the bowl, leaving small drops of the blue glass adhered in some regularly spaced design that circles the bowl (Fig. 195). These dots are added at the same stage (Fig. 125, Number 6) at which you made the blue spiral in your last goblet. The dots are completely fused in, and the goblet finished as before.

Next you might choose to tackle some more complicated additions of blue thread to achieve a design of your own, always adding such design at the same stage as before. Once you have learned how to use your snake thread, feel free as the wind to turn your imagination loose in the matter of color design.

My pictures and sketches are for your guidance and encouragement—not to be thought of as models to be copied. Following, however, are some notes on techniques used in making Figs. 194 to 205.

Figure 194 is decorated with spaced additions from a color snake thread "twist," and solid color thread markings.

Figure 195 has a circle of spaced additions from colored "twist."

Figure 196 has a spiral design of color thread added at stage 3, Fig. 125, hence the color design appears in the stem as well as the bowl.

Figure 197 has a spiral design fused in at stage 6, Fig. 125.

Figure 198 has a flat disc of solid color glass and two small spheres between the hollow stem and the foot.

Figure 199 was ornamented with alternate drops of milk-white and pale blue (or green) and circled with colored "twist."

196

FIGURE 194.

FIGURE 195.

FIGURE 196.

FIGURE 197.

FIGURE 198.

FIGURE 199.

FIGURE 200.   FIGURE 201.   FIGURE 202.

Figure 200 was designed as a stirrup cup—used in olden times to speed the guest after he mounted his horse. It also makes an excellent toastmaster's cup. It stands 7 inches tall, and is decorated with an "all-seeing eye," in milk-white, blue and black iris and pupil, and black line edging, somewhat in the manner of the ancient Egyptian "eye of Horus."

Figure 201 was designed as a "loving cup" for an engagement or wedding gift. The dots are water-white, milk-white, and pale sapphire blue. Generally, one bowl is larger than the other. The lover drinks from the larger bowl, and his lady from the smaller. I call it a "diabolo glass."

Figure 202 stands 8 inches tall—a real ceremonial piece, multi-colored. Gain some experience before you tackle this one.

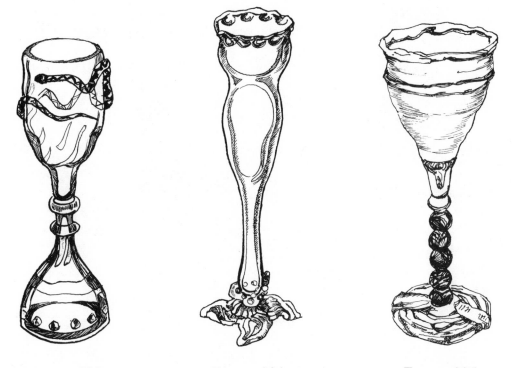

FIGURE 203.   FIGURE 204.   FIGURE 205.

Figure 203 is a goblet circled by a red-eyed snake made of green "twist." The snake coils are left in bas-relief, though thoroughly fused to the bowl. The base is hollow.

Figure 204 is a rose-tinted form with a delicate built-up four-petal foot.

Figure 205 has a stem consisting of small blue-tinted spheres of solid glass, all fused together.

FIGURE 206. Extremely rare glass object by Giacomo Verzelini—1583. *Courtesy, The Corning Museum of Glass, Corning, N. Y.*

FIGURE 207. Goblet with stem in the form of the letters "CE" for Charles XI and Ulrica Eleonora of Sweden (Kungsholm Glass Works, before 1693). *Courtesy, The Corning Museum of Glass, Corning, N. Y.*

FIGURE 208. English goblet and cover (late 17th century). *Courtesy, Victoria & Albert Museum, London, Crown Copyright.*

FIGURE 209. Goblets by J. F. Amelung, New Bremen, Md. (1793).
Courtesy, The Corning Museum of Glass, Corning, N. Y.

CHAPTER 15

Cigarette Holders

Follow the same techniques as described for making a goblet. The cigarette-holder bowls, however, should be bigger, the stems and feet wider, the whole piece stouter throughout. Color your designs to fit table and other decor (see Fig. 210). Such a piece can be used also as a candle-holder (Fig. 231).

FIGURE 210. Cigarette holders.

CHAPTER 16

Spark Lamps

To make a miniature of the kind of lamp used in Colonial days, attach a stout stem of solid glass to a large bubble, exactly opposite its opening. Add a substantial wide foot, using goblet foot technique.

A perforated metal cap (silver is best) shaped to fit the opening in the bubble holds a round wick which draws up the oil. When lighted, this spark lamp gives about as much light as two matches, and also gives off smoke! No wonder that the pioneers retired early.

CHAPTER 17

Muddlers and Stirrers

These are made by adding designs in color to the ends of solid rods, of desired diameter (generally ½ inch) and length. Long stirrers for use in tall mixing jugs can be made from rods having a wider diameter. The plain end, which does the stirring, must be round, fire-polished, and cooled slowly to avoid cracking. (See the color insert.)

The carbon-faced tweezers shown in Fig. 212 make a most valuable tool for helping to form both solid and hollow glass forms. They can be purchased from Bethlehem Apparatus International Co., Inc., Front & Depot Streets, Hellertown, Pa. 18055, as can carbon sticks of various diameters.

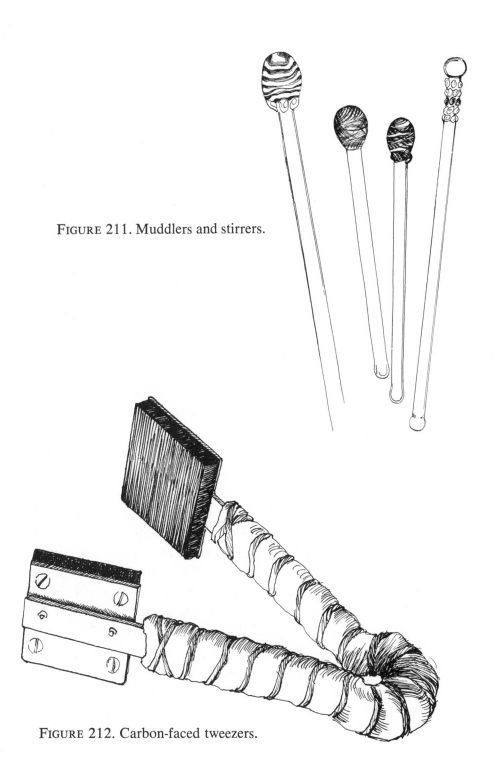

FIGURE 211. Muddlers and stirrers.

FIGURE 212. Carbon-faced tweezers.

CHAPTER 18

Complex Glass Sculptures

The principal tools of the sculptor in glass are his torch flames. These vary between a sharp needle flame and wide "brush" flames, and are used to soften solid glass so that it can be squeezed and shaped with a variety of simple brass tools and tweezers, rolled and shaped on the marver, or formed by dexterous twisting while the piece is hot enough, and therefore soft enough, to come under the forming influence of gravity.

Sculpture must be considered work for the advanced student since it requires all the knowledge and skills previously acquired. Of first importance is a sound working knowledge of how solid glass behaves under the influence of gravity when heated well above its softening point. This knowledge, and the manual skill to use it, will indicate which of several techniques will best serve to fashion the piece as desired. The pull of gravity on the slow flowing mass will always be a major factor, while the correct choice of tools for dexterous manipulation must play an equally important part in the drama of forming this magical substance according to your intention.

Essential also is a thorough mastery of the skills required to fuse

208

two elements of a sculpture together successfully and to allow the junction between them to cool to room temperature without cracking. The pigmented design of the separate elements, prior to fusion into the total design of the sculpture, will require a marshaling of all the experience gained in making previous color designed pieces.

Nothing short of a slow-motion moving picture could adequately convey every detail of the many steps necessary to form a glass sculpture. Lengthy descriptions do not suffice—so, plunge in, armed with the major hints I have given, and you will quickly learn, by your mistakes as much as your successes, to translate your own conceptions of form into three-dimensional reality. All the sketches of sculptured pieces have been made from my own original creations.

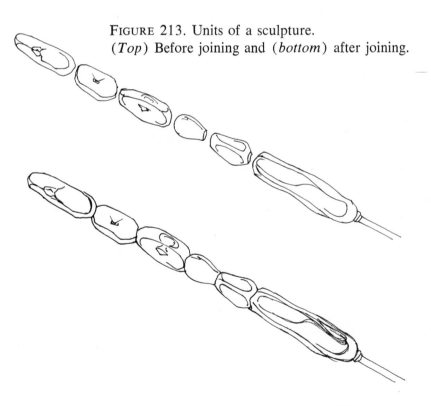

FIGURE 213. Units of a sculpture.
(*Top*) Before joining and (*bottom*) after joining.

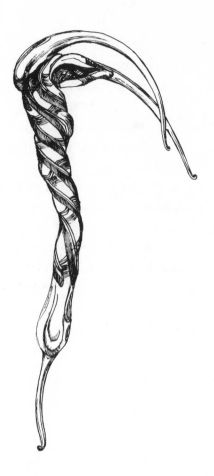

FIGURE 215.

FIGURE 214.

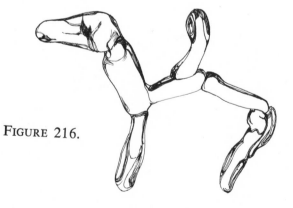

FIGURE 216.

210

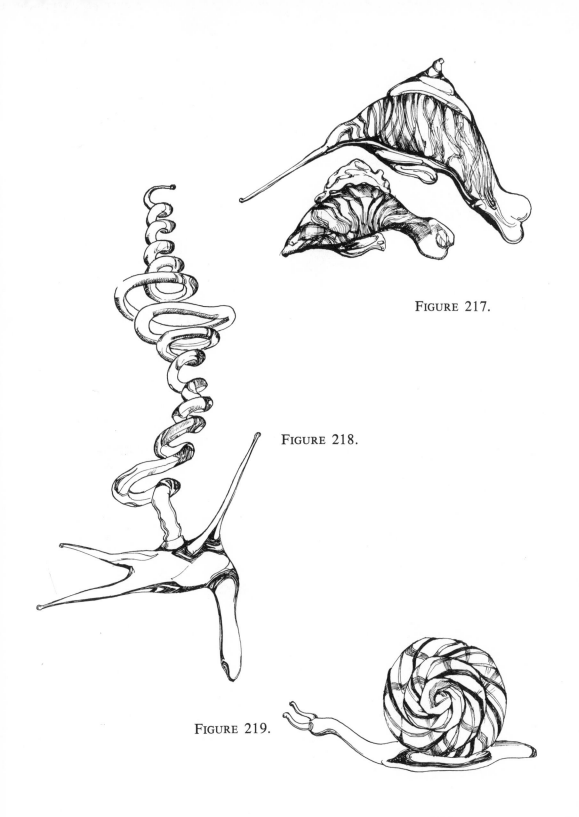

FIGURE 217.

FIGURE 218.

FIGURE 219.

211

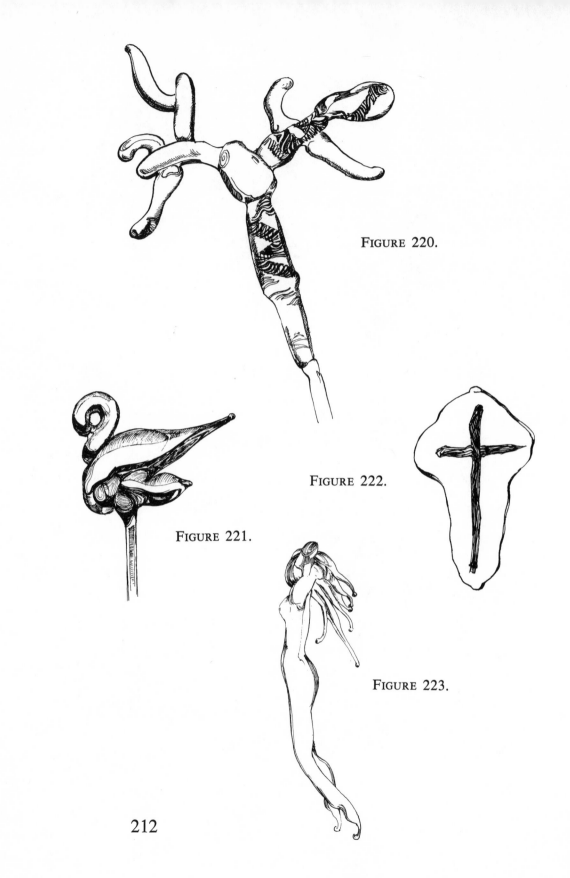

FIGURE 220.

FIGURE 222.

FIGURE 221.

FIGURE 223.

212

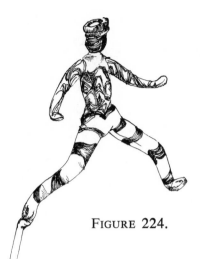

FIGURE 224.

FIGURE 225.

FIGURE 227.

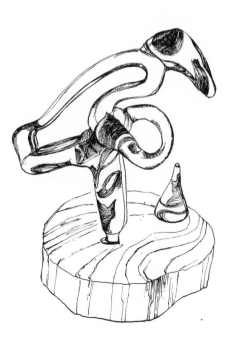

FIGURE 226.

FIGURE 228.

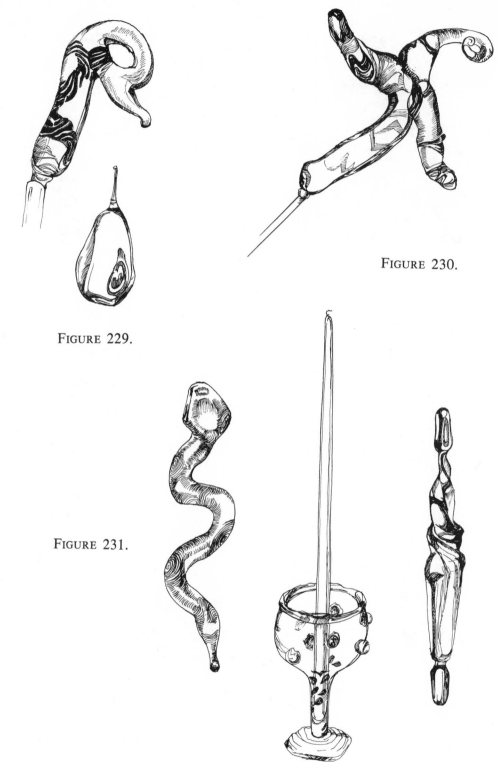

FIGURE 229.

FIGURE 230.

FIGURE 231.

214

CHAPTER 19

Bottles, Carafes, Flasks, Jugs, Cruets,

Figure 125, Numbers 1–8, shows the successive steps to take in making larger pieces of blown hollow ware. Quite naturally, the larger the piece to be made, the more additions of 5-mm. rod coils must be added in order to maintain a stout wall in the expanding piece.

Figures 232–237 show some pieces still on their blowpipes. Study all these pictures carefully. Do not, at first, be too ambitious in the matter of size. Practice, with its successes and failures, will be your best teacher, and will soon reward your efforts. But quality rather than quantity should always remain your goal as you progress in size. It is better to make excellent smaller pieces than poor larger ones!

ADDING HANDLES

To be quite certain that handles are completely fused to the necks or bodies of pieces of hollow ware (if only partially fused they are almost certain to crack), it is best to fuse two blobs of glass at the

FIGURE 232.

FIGURE 233.

FIGURE 234.

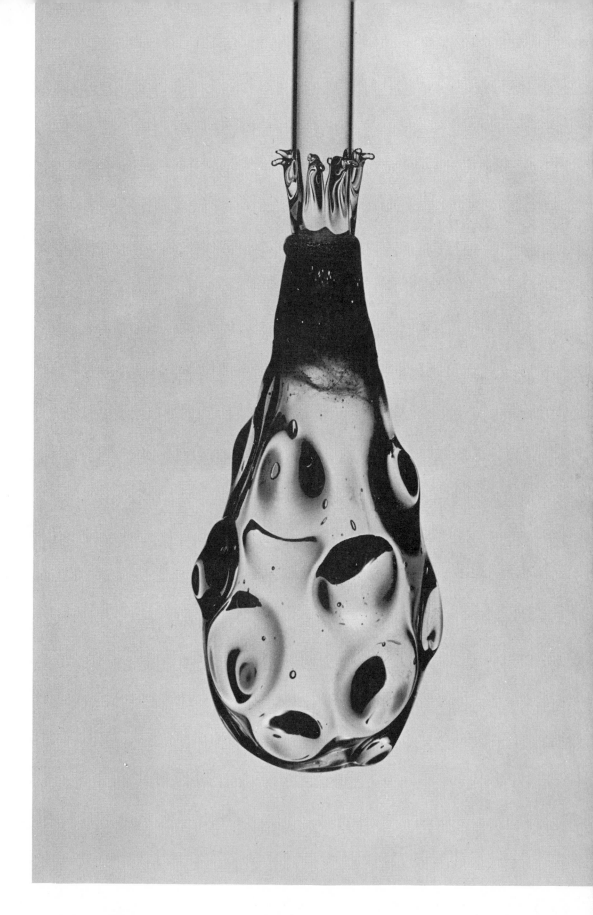

FIGURE 235.

FIGURE 236.

FIGURE 237.

FIGURE 238. Spanish vase (16th century). *Courtesy, Victoria & Albert Museum, London, Crown Copyright.*

FIGURE 239. The Hornet and Peacock Decanter, Birmingham Glass
Works of Charles Ihmsen, Pittsburgh, Pa. (c. 1813). *Courtesy, The
Corning Museum of Glass, Corning, N. Y.*

FIGURE 241. Bank—free blown. Sandwich, Mass. (c. 1825–1850).
Courtesy, The Corning Museum of Glass, Corning, N. Y.

FIGURE 242. French vase (late 19th century). *Courtesy, Victoria & Albert Museum, London, Crown Copyright.*

FIGURE 243. Encased and acid-etched vase by Emile Galle, Nancy, France (c. 1885–1900). *Courtesy, The Corning Museum of Glass, Corning, N. Y.*

FIGURE 245. French vases of clear free-blown and acid-etched glass by Maurice Marinot (*left*, 1929; *right*, 1934). *Courtesy, The Corning Museum of Glass, Corning, N.Y.*

points to which the handle is to be attached, as shown in Fig. 246. This can easily be done with a fine flame without distorting the neck or body of the piece. Once properly fused in, these two excrescences can then be joined together with the glass that is to be formed into the handle.

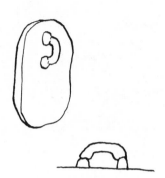

FIGURE 246.

The entire area of the piece should be heated to an even dull red—not so hot as to cause distortion—before the two blobs are adhered, while adding the glass for the handles, and during the shaping of the handles with tweezers and carbon stick. Then, be sure that the whole area is cooled as slowly as possible, first by gradually turning the oxygen lower in several stages, and then finishing off in the carbon flame and the asbestos-lined container.

BASES

Perhaps the most effective base for a simple spherical vase or bottle is made by heating the extreme end area, while it is still on the blowpipe, and pressing it onto the marver. The blowpipe of course must be at right angles to the marver surface for this operation.

Many variants of this procedure involve circling the base end with 5-mm. rod or colored snake thread, fusing in, and flattening as before. Complex bases can readily be built up according to your taste. Here are some of the more simple suggestions (Fig. 247). Whatever base you choose to make, be certain that the area around it is returned to the torch after marvering, and heated to a dull red, taking care not to distort the piece, before gradual cooling to room temperature. Remember that the solid glass of the handle is always much thicker than the wall to which it is fused. This means that it will tend to cool more slowly than the wall. Hence the cooling must be slow enough to keep the wall warm and allow the handle to cool to the same temperature. Unless this process is rigidly adhered to, cracking is always a danger.

FIGURE 247. Bases.

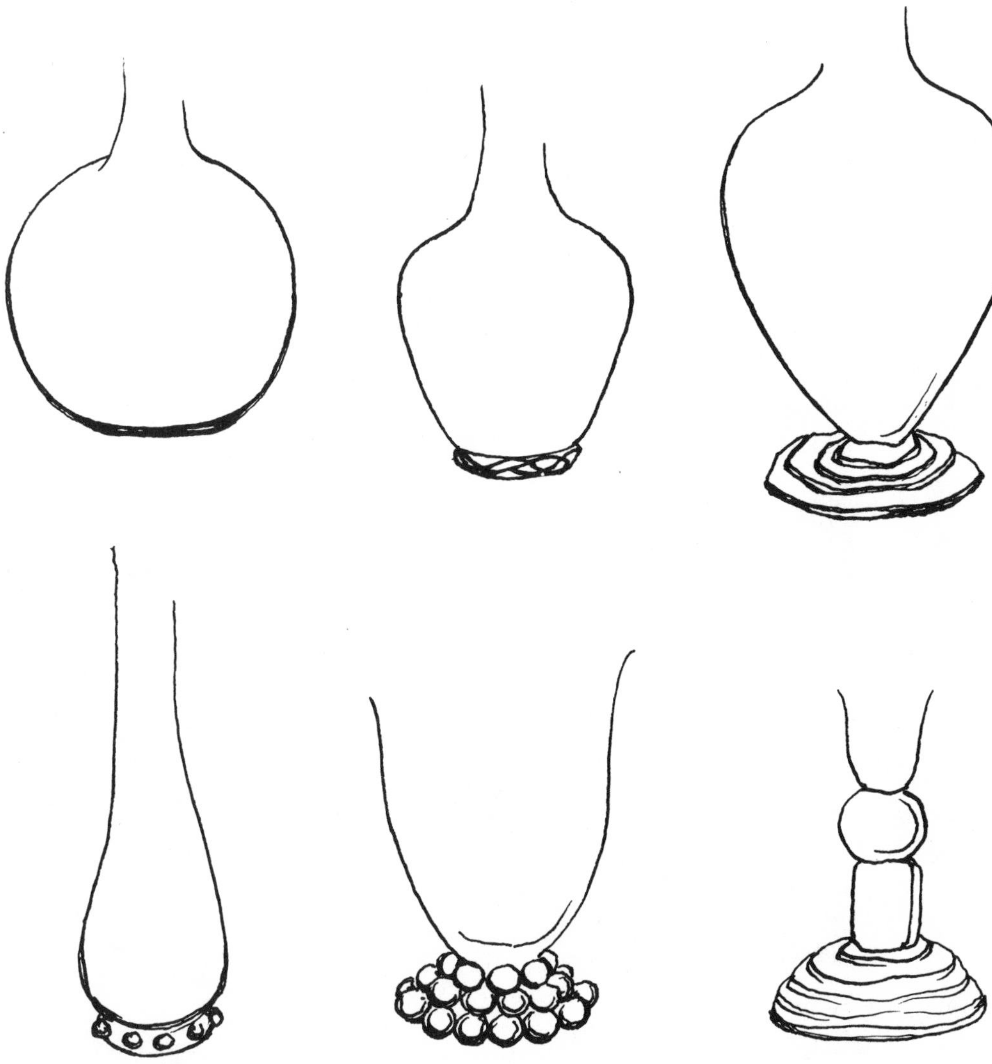

231

For sketches of eleven of my pieces, see Figs. 248–258. The long decorated necks of Figs. 248–251, 254, and 257 are made in the following manner.

The first three steps (Figs. 259–261) are self-explanatory. Figure 262 shows an area near the blowpipe of the stout-walled decorated bubble being softened in the flame. A 5-mm. rod has been attached to the end of the bubble. The neck is now pulled out evenly, while holding the piece perpendicular to achieve the result

FIGURE 248.　　　　FIGURE 249.　　　　FIGURE 250.

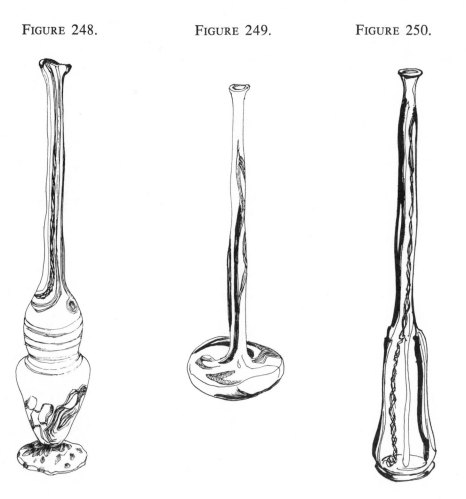

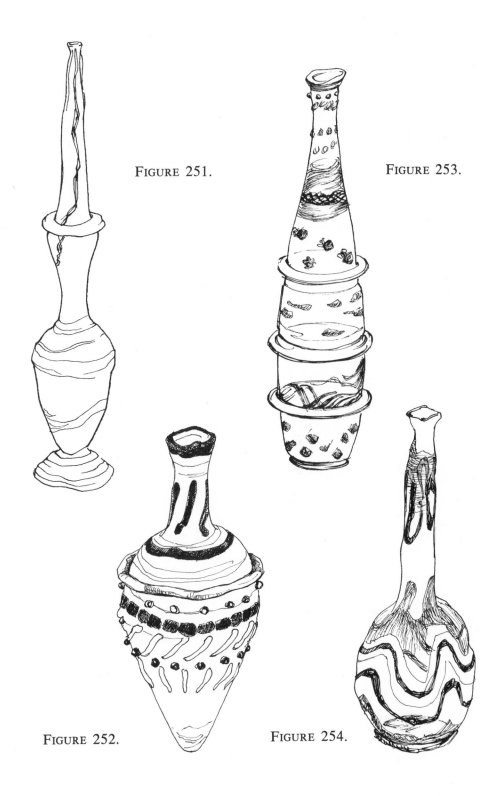

FIGURE 251.

FIGURE 253.

FIGURE 252.

FIGURE 254.

233

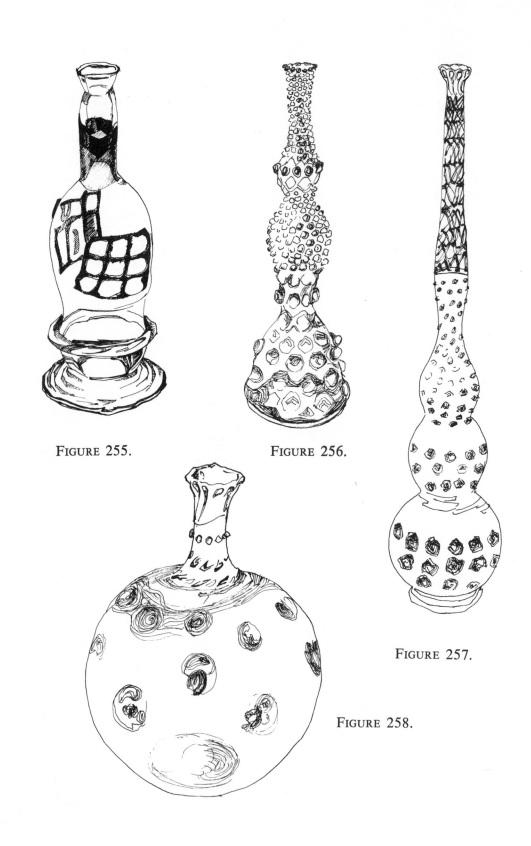

FIGURE 255.

FIGURE 256.

FIGURE 257.

FIGURE 258.

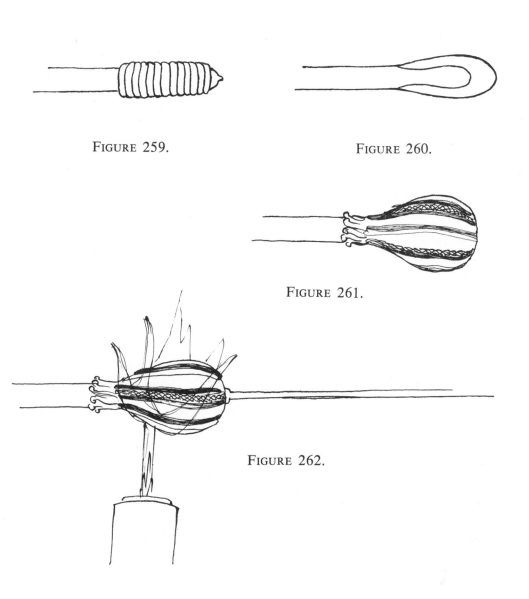

FIGURE 259.

FIGURE 260.

FIGURE 261.

FIGURE 262.

shown in Fig. 263, and, after further heating, Fig. 264. Figure 265 shows the completed piece, still on the blowpipe, after further addition of glass and more blowing.

Figure 266 shows a piece with four "waists." This narrowing of a blown piece is best achieved by the steps labeled A, B, C, D, E

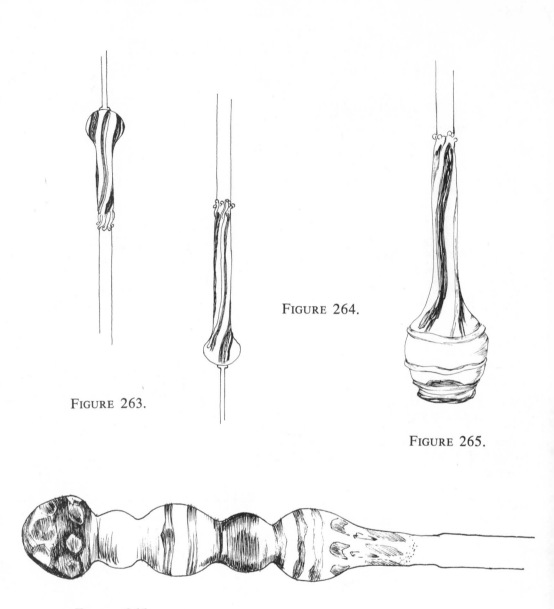

FIGURE 263.

FIGURE 264.

FIGURE 265.

FIGURE 266.

in Fig. 267. The extreme tip of A is heated, and blown gently to form B. Glass coils are added, as in C; D shows the coils fused; and E is the result of further blowing. Add more glass as needed for further enlargement. Some of my work may be seen in Figs. 268–280.

236

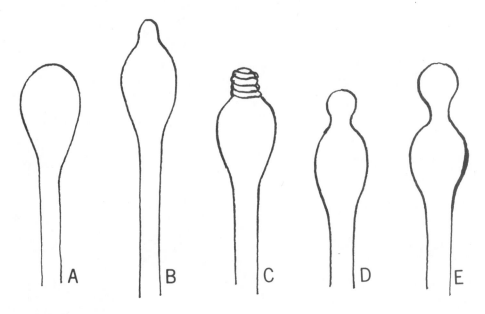

FIGURE 267.

FIGURE 268.

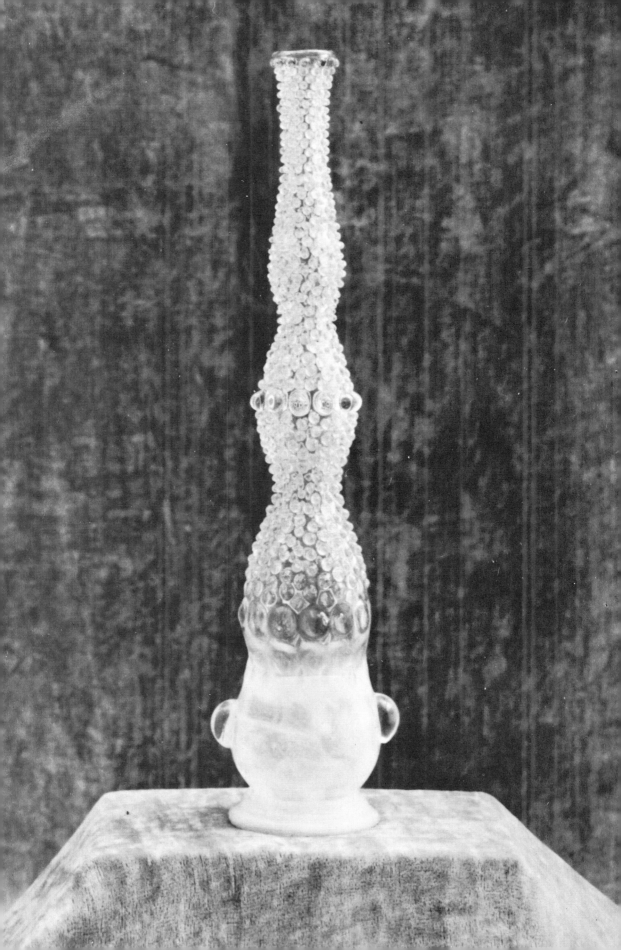

FIGURE 270.

FIGURE 269.

FIGURE 272.

FIGURE 271.

FIGURE 274.

FIGURE 273.

FIGURE 275.

FIGURE 276.

FIGURE 277.

FIGURE 278.

FIGURE 279.

FIGURE 280.

MINIATURE BOTTLES

Figures 282 and 283 show pieces 2 to 3 inches tall. Some are blue, some green, some have designs in milk-white snake thread. They are blown on blowpipes narrowed beforehand to form the necks. They are particularly effective when shown in groupings.

FIGURE 282.

FIGURE 281. Islamic bottle made in Persia (11th or 12th century). Decorated with elaborate network of pinchered and trailed handles; surmounted with free-blown figures of animals or abstract horned beasts. *Courtesy, The Corning Museum of Glass, Corning, N. Y.*

251

FIGURE 283.

STOPPERS

A stopper for a perfume bottle penetrates a cork which has been selected to fit the neck of the individual bottle. The long rod is used as an applicator. Infinite possibilities in design, color, and length are yours. The hole in the cork can be made by a special reamer or by burning with a red-hot instrument to the desired diameter. The stopper can then be cemented to the cork, if desired. (See Fig. 284.)

252

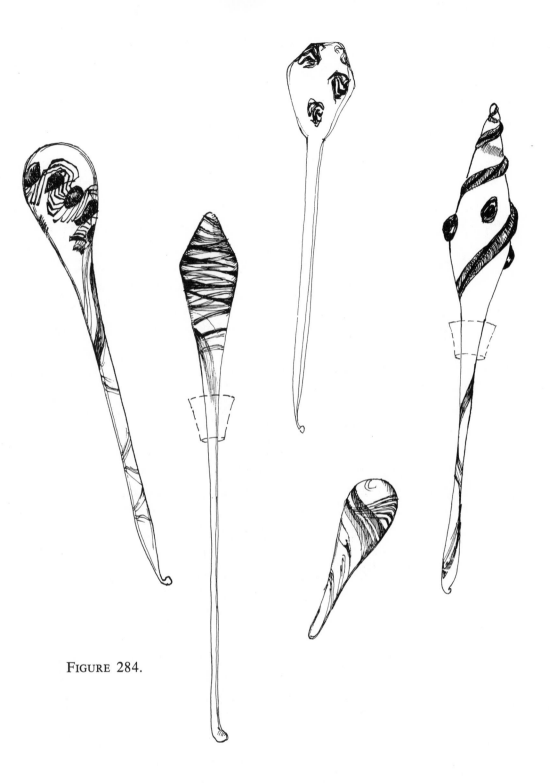

FIGURE 284.

253

CHAPTER 20

Floating Bubbles

Beautiful decorative arrangements can be made by floating a number of bubbles, varying in size, among flowers and reeds in a glass tray or bowl. The bubbles can be colored or clear, or covered with snake thread designs, and should be blown on the end of a thin drawn-out blowpipe. The hole should be sealed after removal from the blowpipe, so as not to admit water.

Fine white sand can be sprinkled on the bottom of the bowl, and bubbles, filled with colored water and then sealed, can be placed on the sand. Diluted vegetable dyes used in cooking may be introduced into the bubbles in the following manner: take a blowpipe and rotate an area in the torch flame 6 inches from the working end, holding the blowpipe at each end. Draw out the heated part to a tube thin enough to fit inside the thin tube attached to the bubble to be filled with colored water. Cut this tube near to the end of the wide blowpipe. Now you have the thin tube (several inches long) attached to the main part of the blowpipe.

Place the thin end into the cup containing the dye, and suck up the liquid until the wide tube is full. Now insert the end of the tube into the neck of the bubble you want to fill, and allow the liquid to flow into it. Leave a small cavity of air on top of the liquid. Seal the neck of the bubble in flame.

254

CHAPTER 21

Touch Pieces

Men and women have always found delight in the sense of touch. Objects made especially for tactile pleasure have been used and treasured by all the old civilizations, and in our modern age we make and enjoy them. Traditionally, such pieces have been made of many materials, such as jade, ivory, rare hardwood—even polished metals. Sometimes, especially in our own hectic times, they are thought of as "tranquilizers," "pacifiers" and the like.

Nothing is smoother to the touch of hands than surfaces of fire-polished glass. I often give glass touch pieces to my sick or nervous friends. They find comfort and relaxation in feeling them. Here's how you can make them!

Begin with a glass rod about 15 inches long, and ¾ inch in diameter. Heat the last 3 inches of one end to a dull red. Pigment this heated piece with any design you wish, by trailing or dotting with colored snake thread. Fuse in the colored design until it is flush with the surface. Now attach a 5-mm. rod to the extreme end, and separate at point A in the torch (Fig. 288). You now hold a globular lump of glass on the end of your 5-mm. rod. I suggest that you keep this shape, heat it to a dull red throughout, then begin gradually to lessen the oxygen supply to your torch until only a yellow carbon flame is burning. Blacken it thoroughly in the

FIGURE 285. Touch pieces.

256

carbon flame, and, while it is still very hot, remove the 5-mm. rod with fine oxygen-propane flame, while holding the body of your piece in tongs covered with asbestos. Still holding it in the tongs, return the piece and the tips of the tongs into the carbon flame to cool still further. Place it in an asbestos-lined tin to cool to room temperature.

Innumerable free forms may be made by using suitable modifications of this technique. Before removing your form from the thick rod, always attach a 5-mm. rod to some part of your creation which will allow you to grip the piece with the tongs and have easy access to the fine flame which you must use to sever connection with the 5-mm. rod.

FIGURE 286. Touch pieces.

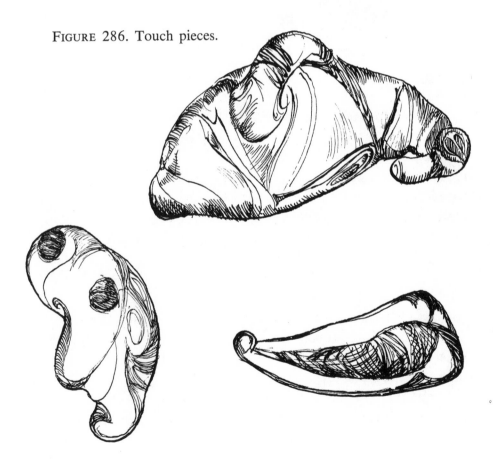

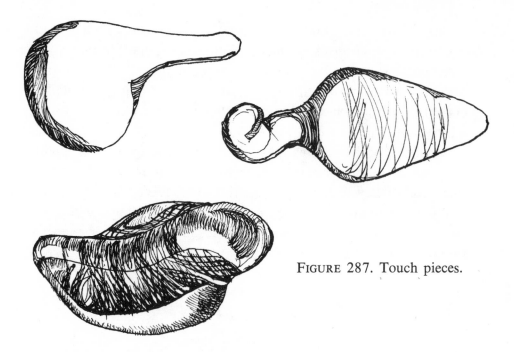

FIGURE 287. Touch pieces.

The color pictures and the sketches of touch pieces that I have made are presented as suggestions for your guidance. A good-sized blob of glass can be molded by gravity, marver, and your tools, and colored according to your fancy, into simple or complex forms. Great care must always be taken to return the whole piece to a dull red throughout before beginning the slow cooling process. Only in this way will pieces of irregular shape and thickness be made safe against cracking.

As I finish writing this last chapter, I find myself hoping that you have gone over certain passages in the book many times, and that they have infused you with some of the unbounded enthusiasm I feel for the creative life, and my special love for the miracle substance we call glass.

I hope that you can hardly wait until tomorrow to run out and make one of the most rewarding purchases of your life, so that you may bring glass into your own home and begin to revel in its transparent beauty, while you learn to mold it after your own imaginative fancy.

Yes, please *do* bring glass into your life and your home! Make a friend of it. Discover how subtle is its behavior as your torch awakens it to flowing life. Form it. Color it. Help it, with your imagination and skillful hands, to assume some of the limitless variety of graceful forms its timeless beauty deserves. You will quickly fall in love with glass.

You, the unique creator, will learn to let yourself flow into your creation. You will discover that, while you thought you were only attending the birth of a new object, *you* have been growing into a new knowledge of yourself. You have been out-picturing a fragment of your inner riches—exfoliating, allowing your life its own unique expression in a medium of unparalleled quality, the very chalice of light and color.

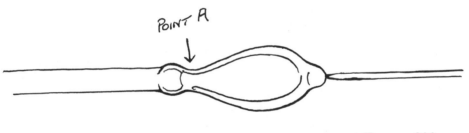

POINT A

FIGURE 288.

You and I, and all men and women and children, are creators—first, last, and all the time—no matter how far we may have been "wronged and prevented from our own," as Emerson put it. We must create to live, for we are nothing less than tiny collaborators with God in the ever-changing, never-ending procession of His mighty and mysterious purposes.

By fostering and exercising our God-given creative talents, we banish fear from our minds and hearts, and doubt no longer why

259

we are here or what we should do. Whether our works are great or small is of no moment. Our inner fountain is playing, flowing freely to the fulfillment of the life that is ours, while, in concert with our fellows, we are learning to create a man-made habitation worthy of the nature cradle which surrounds and supports us. Worthy, because it is in harmony with, and a part of, the master creation of the universe.

Epilogue

A small boy wandering down a golden corridor of heaven stopped in front of a door marked: DO NOT DISTURB! Noting his curiosity, a passing Saint whispered in his ear, "You may peep in just for a moment."

There sat an august figure, engaged in molding some small object in His hands.

"What is He making?" asked the boy.

"That is God," replied the Saint. "He is fashioning the hind leg of a flea."

Thoughts for
Creative Minds

Saint Francis of Assisi

He who works with his hands is a laborer.

He who works with his hands and his head is a craftsman.

He who works with his hands and his head and his heart is an artist.

William James

The great use of a life is to spend it for something that outlasts it.

Ralph Waldo Emerson

A man is only half of himself, the other half is his work.

Every man is at last an artist, no matter how far he may be wronged and prevented from his own.

262

RABINDRANATH TAGORE

Joy without play is no play at all—play without activity is no play. Activity is the play of joy.

The more man acts and makes actual what was latent in him, the nearer does he bring the distant "Yet-to-be."

LEONARDO DA VINCI

A man can have neither a greater nor a less dominion than that over himself.

MARTIN LUTHER

If I believed the world were to end tomorrow, I would still plant a tree today.

CONFUCIUS

It is better to light one small candle than curse the darkness.

JUSTICE HOLMES

No one can cut new paths in company. He must do that alone.

MICHELANGELO

Trifles make perfection—and perfection is no trifle.

WILLIAM MORRIS

There are two things more precious to men than any other—hopeful work and fearless rest. If you know how to provide these two things, you know all there is to know about politics. If you know how to prepare men to enjoy these two things, you know all there is to know about education. If you know what these two blessings ultimately mean, you know all you will ever know about religion.

ELBERT HUBBARD

One machine can do the work of fifty ordinary men. No machine can do the work of one extraordinary man.

WILLIAM JAMES

To kill time is not murder. It is suicide.

HENRY DAVID THOREAU

If you have built castles in the air, your work need not be lost: that is where they should be. Now put the foundations under them.

Only that day dawns to which we are awake.

WILLIAM SHAKESPEARE

Thought, to be worthwhile, must complete itself in action.

SAMUEL BUTLER

Life is like playing a violin solo in public, and learning the instrument as one goes.

JONATHAN SWIFT

May you live all the days of your life!

JOHN STUART MILL

Ideologies divide. Projects unite.

THOMAS A. EDISON

The pleasure of idleness is one of the great superstitions of the world.

SAMUEL BUTLER

All of the animals except man know that the principal business of life is to enjoy it.

FROM THE HINDU

Pitiful is the one who, fearing failure, makes no beginning.

RALPH WALDO EMERSON

See how the mass of men worry themselves into nameless graves, while here and there some great unselfish soul forgets himself into immortality.

MARK TWAIN

If you cannot stand solitude, perhaps you bore others too.

Selected Bibliography

Buckley, Wilfred. *The Art of Glass*. New York, 1939.

———. *European Glass*. Boston and New York, 1926.

Dillon, Edward. *Glass*. New York, Putnam; London, Methuen, 1907.

Elville, E. M. *The Collector's Dictionary of Glass*. London, Country Life, Ltd., 1961.

Glass from the Ancient World: The Ray Winfield Smith Collection. The Corning Museum of Glass, Corning, N. Y., 1957.

Glass from the Corning Museum of Glass. Corning, N. Y., 1958.

Haynes, E. Barrington. *Glass Through the Ages*. Harmondsworth, Middlesex, Penguin Books, 1959.

Honey, William Bowyer. *Glass: A Handbook for the Study of Glass Vessels of All Periods and Countries and a Guide to the Museum Collections*. (Victoria and Albert Museum.) London, Ministry of Education, 1946.

Perrot, Paul. *Three Great Centuries of Venetian Glass*. The Corning Museum of Glass, Corning, N. Y., 1958.

266

Suggested Reading

General Works:

Barrelet, James. *La Verrerie en France de l'Époque Gallo-Romaine à Nos Jours*. Paris, Librairie Larousse, 1935.

Frothingham, Alice Wilson. *Hispanic Glass, with Examples in the Collection of the Hispanic Society of America*. New York, 1941.

Glass 1959: A Special Exhibition of International Contemporary Glass. The Corning Museum of Glass, Corning, N. Y., 1959.

Janneau, Guillaume. *Modern Glass*. London, The Studio Limited; New York, William Edwin Rudge, 1931.

Stennett-Willson, R. *The Beauty of Modern Glass*. London, The Studio Limited; New York, Studio Publications, Inc., 1948.

Thorpe, W. A. *English Glass*. London, A. & C. Black, 1935.

General Works on American Glass:

Daniel, Dorothy. *Cut and Engraved Glass*. New York, M. Barrows, 1950.

Knittle, Rhea. *Early American Glass*. New York, Century, 1927.

Lee, Ruth Webb. *Early American Pressed Glass*. Northboro, Mass., 1931.

————. *Nineteenth Century Art Glass*. New York, M. Barrows, 1952.

————. *Victorian Glass*. Northboro, Mass., 1944.

McKearin, George S. and Helen. *American Glass*. New York, Crown, 1941.

————. *Two Hundred Years of American Blown Glass*. New York, 1950.

Revi, A. C. *Nineteenth Century Glass—Its Genesis and Development*. New York, Nelson, 1959.

Watkins, Lura Woodside. *American Glass and Glassmaking*. New York, Chanticleer Press, 1950.

Special Subjects:

Bergstrom, Evangeline H. *Old Glass Paperweights*. Chicago, Lakeside Press, 1940.

Comstock, Helen. *The Concise Encyclopedia of American Antiques*. New York, Hawthorn, 1958.

Freeman, Larry. *Iridescent Glass*. Watkins Glen, N. Y., Century House, 1956.

Harrington, J. C. *Glassmaking at Jamestown, America's First Industry*. Richmond, Va., Dietz Press, 1952.

Hunter, Frederick William. *Stiegel Glass*. Boston, Houghton Mifflin, 1914. (To be read *after* McKearin: *Two Hundred Years of American Blown Glass*. Valuable sources, but conclusions not up to present scholarship.)

Innes, Lowell. *Early Glass of the Pittsburgh District*. Pittsburgh, Carnegie Museum, 1949.

Jefferson, Josephine. *Wheeling Glass*. Westfield, N. Y., Guide Publishing Company, 1958.

Lee, Ruth Webb. *Sandwich Glass*. Framingham Centre, Mass., 1939.

Lee, Ruth Webb, and James H. Rose. *American Glass Cup Plates*. Northboro, Mass., 1948.

Suggested Reading

McKearin, Helen. *The Story of American Historical Flasks*. The Corning Museum of Glass, Corning, N. Y., 1953.

Metz, Alice Hulett. *Early American Pattern Glass*. Westfield, N. Y., Guide Publishing Company, 1958.

Millford, Harriet N. "Amelung and His New Bremen Glasswares," *Maryland Historical Magazine*, XLVII (March, 1952), pp. 1–10.

Smith, Francis Edgar. *American Glass Paperweights*. Wallaston, Mass., The Antique Press, 1939.

Van Rensselaer, Stephen. *Early American Bottles and Flasks*. Peterborough, N. H., 1926.

Periodicals Containing Useful Information About American Glass:

Antique Journal

Antiques

Hobbies

Journal of Glass Studies

Spinning Wheel

Index

271

John Burton

John Burton was born and reared in Yorkshire, England. His father was a steel man and he apprenticed Burton to chemists in a steel factory in Sheffield. There he acquired a practical knowledge of chemistry and metallurgy. Subsequently, he joined the staff of the research laboratories of Cammell, Laird & Company, naval architects and shipbuilders for the British Admiralty. He worked there in positions of increasing responsibility during World War I and married at this time.

Gradually Mr. Burton became dissatisfied with his work. The horrors of the war had their effect on him. He no longer wanted to be associated with the production of weapons and he resolved to change his life.

Working in the laboratories, he had acquired considerable skill in the making and mending of the complicated glass apparatus. This was the beginning of a lifelong preoccupation. In 1921 Mr. Burton made his break with Cammell, Laird & Company and became co-founder of the Sheffield Educational Settlement where he served as Director of Arts and Crafts. The combined creative experiences of working with his hands and teaching others proved